A brief rambling report as my memory permits
A sort of history of

HONITON POTTERY

Mostly of 1961 to 1992.
Put together to placate my family.
Hopefully to be of some help
should anyone wish to research
the happenings at a small country pottery.
The historical events,
the range of items made,
how the pottery was made and
the very valuable staff who made everything possible.
by

Paul Redvers

with the help of the family
especially Jennie for
adding valuable memories and helping with the presentation.
My sincere thanks to all who contributed.

Published by Colin R Wright, Egland, Honiton, Devon, EX14 3NW

Part 1

A little history.
Pages 6-27

Part 2

A tour of the Pottery production.
Pages 29-47

Part 3

The various Products and Designers.
Pages 48-63

Part 4

Just some of the potters.
Pages 64-70

Appendix
Pricelists and other records.
Pages 71-87

Glossary
Pottery terms.
88 onwards and
Notes on the property.

———————————————

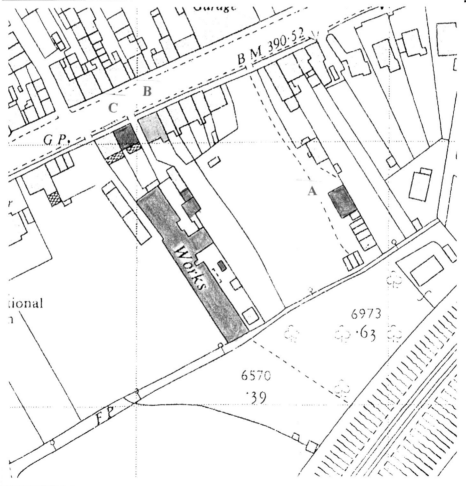

With permission reproduced from Ordnance Survey Map December 1958

A   Noted as "The Old Pottery"
B   No 30 Kingswood, High Street.
C   No 32 Montpellier, High Street

Some early records of Pottery in Honiton
and
My memories from 1961 to the 1990's

On January 1st. 1961 Jennie and I arrived to take over and run the Pottery in Honiton while Philip Cowell, the new Company Chairman, and his wife Nora as non-executive directors remained in London.   We discovered that we were to become part of a long tradition of pottery making in the town.   The earliest records seem to be in 1643 in the Honiton Churchwarden's Accounts. Volume 29, pages 225 & 227 mention pottery making.   I believe items were made for the Church.

A poll taken on the 21st November 1763 at the house of John Barnes, within the Borough of Honiton" record....

Samuel Ford, Master Potter	William Flood, Potter
Thomas Brooke, Potter	Isaac Collins, Potter
Charles Denham, Potter	John Linnington, Potter

On the 14th November 1775 James Rogers, was brought before the Justice of the Peace at Honiton and the document recording his examination states:- James Rogers, residing at Honiton, potter, was originally apprenticed to John Beavis, of Dornes, in the Parish of Illminster, and afterwards by assignment in writing to John Norris of Donyard (sic), potter: when aged 19 ran away to Honiton and resided with John Flood, potter, for one month and afterwards with Samuel Ford, potter, as labourer."   James Rogers was born in 1747 and died in 1829.

In 1791 The "British Directory" mentions potters at Honiton named Samuel Ford and Humphrey Ford.

In 1830 Pigot & Co. Directory names two potters of High Street, Honiton - Thomas Flood and Peter Hussey.

In 1838 Robson's Directory notes a Thomas Flood Potter.   In 1840 it notes Thomas Flood potter in High Street and Peter Hussey also in High Street.

The 1842 Tythe Map shows Thomas Flood's pottery, Ref. 389, in the High Street opposite the entrance to Dowell Street and Peter Hussey's "The Old Pottery"... former Kiln buildings... comprises Tithe numbers 719, 720, 722, 723 and 724 behind 18 High Street. It is marked on the 1887 map as 'Pottery'.

In 1850 White's Directory for Honiton notes a Pottery making brown Earthenware, and notes Susan Hussey, potter. In 1857 there was a Joseph Pyne, potter in the High Street and the 1866 Post Office Directory gives Francis Copp as a "brown Earthenware potter" of High Street.

The Census of 1871 names potters, Francis & Lucy Copp at 4, High Street, James Greenslade at 11, High Street, William Willicott at 15, High Street and Henry Ash at 37, High Street.

In 1878/9 White's Devonshire Directory lists a Pottery making brown earthenware in Honiton.

In 1878 Harrods Royal County Directory shows Copp, F, Brownware Manufacturer.

The Census 1881 names potters Richard Raymond at 9, High Street, James Greenslade at 11, High Street and William Willicott at 21, High Street.

Now we come to the 1890 Whites Directory where James Webber, Earthenware Potter, High Street is mentioned. There are records of him selling his wares in Exeter. James Webber died in April 1920. Little is known about the early potters except the Hussey appears on deeds relating to the Honiton Pottery site. I can only assume the others were employees.

1916-18 are believed to be the dates for Forster and Hunt who, it is said, took over from James Webber. Pottery produced by them is the earliest identifiable pottery made in Honiton. See The Honiton Pottery Collectors Newsletter No 41. Ellis Sidney Forster, born in 1886 came from Burslem, Staffordshire and was part of a family of potters. He was in financial difficulties in 1914 or 1915 because it is noted that he had to make a Deed of Arrangement to pay various suppliers in Honiton and Stoke. He lived at Montpellier, 34. High Street and he married Ada Thomas in Honiton in 1919.

Most of the details from 1918 are included in the Collard book by Carol Cashmore but it might be interesting to note a few things. The "Old Pottery Site" is mentioned in a document relating to the land behind Nos. 16, 18 and 20 High Street. The land behind 20 to 28 High Street, the old Pottery and kiln buildings (noted on my map as **A**) were given to Mrs Slade in the will of her husband dated May 1950.

The pottery site in the 1920s was behind No 32 High Street, known as Henrietta Cottage. This house was later known as Montpellier (noted on my map as **C**) which with the "walled garden at the back of the house and the large linney at the back of Mr. Oake's garden", was left by Richard Sprague to his daughter Ellen Webber, wife of James Webber. Montpellier was sold to Charles Collard in 1922.

In July 1924, Ethel Maud Parrett sold Kingswood, 30 High Street to Walter Howard for £600. In August 1928 Kingswood was purchased by Charles Collard, as his home where he lived with his daughter Joan. It was conveyed to Honiton Art Potteries in June 1947. This eventually became the Honiton Pottery Shop having been sold in the mean time to Mr Pannell and re-purchased by the Honiton Pottery in 1963.

Records show that the pottery was owned by Norman Hull, Nancy Hull, Harry Barrett and Phyllis Barrett from 1947 when Charles Collard and Joan retired. In 1947 Harry and Phyllis Barratt sold their interest to William and Edith Chapplow. They were already in business in the town owning the Honiton China Shop at 100, High Street and a wholesale china business in King Street.

There were major changes from the Pottery of Charles Collard's time where hand throwing was the basic production method. The Hulls introduced the commercial slip casting and

8

jollying as used in Stoke on Trent . A Stoke mould maker, Tom Sherrif, made most of the master moulds based on Collard shapes. However he left Honiton Pottery in the late 1950's and started The Axe Cliff Pottery at Beer, where he produced similar shapes. The end products had cream glaze outside and a pastel colour inside, rather like Poole Pottery. Some were hand painted, though not with Collard designs, but many were transfer decorated.

Norman Hull subsequently left leaving Nancy Hull in the business with William and Edith Chapplow running the pottery. The Collard designs had been adapted and were being very skilfully made and well painted.

The "Clean Air Act" of 1956 made the use of the two bottle, coal fired, kilns illegal. The circles where the kilns had been were still obvious in the kiln area. Four special new 'Trolley hearth' electric kilns made by Cromartie Kilns of Stoke were their replacements. They were each rated to use 60 KW per hour.

This heavy electric load required a large 3 phase supply and special meters to use the 'Cheap rate' off peak electricity. The cost of firing kilns in Stoke on Trent was much lower because coal gas kilns were used. As Devon had no coal, gas was very expensive in Honiton. The new trolley hearth kilns were more convenient . The trolley trucks were loaded and unloaded outside the kiln. There were several spare trucks which could be loaded ready for firing as necessary. This was very helpful when we were busy. To load a Bottle kiln a person had to get inside it. After firing the kiln had to cool down completely before unloading and reloading which took several days.

In 1961 I arrived and Bill Chapplow was to show me the ropes while Nancy Hull looked after the office. The Pottery consisted of the "Works" buildings as noted on the plan on the title page. It did not include any of the houses on the High Street.

The Pottery was approached by a steep narrow drive between Nos. 30 and 32 High Street. A flat sign in dark paint stretched between the buildings at the High Street. It was some years before we had a sign approved, protruding over the street.

The entrance was through corrugated iron gates which were mounted on brick pillars surmounted by marble busts, which, incidentally, had no relevance to the Pottery' but looked quite impressive. Any area which was painted was in a dark maroon colour giving a very sombre impression.

The Directors' office and the showroom/shop was a shed joining the back of the garage of No. 30 High Street. The showroom was made of corrugated iron with a thin sheet of fibreboard lining. It was very cold in winter. It was from this showroom on the site that all our retail sales were made. We took £5 in total during Christmas week in 1961!   Fortunately Bill and Edith Chapplow in their China Shop did sell our Honiton pottery products.

The Pottery was an odd hotchpotch of buildings.   There was the central kiln area with two ex-army Nissan type huts one up and one down from the area.   Beside the kiln area was the old coal shed and a packing shed.

There was a central heating boiler which inadequately heated a few sections of the Pottery. The packing shed had no heating so, in winter when packing was needed the packer usually stood in a box of straw to keep his feet warm!   It was surprising to remember there were so very few complaints about the conditions.   As the years went by the conditions did improve.   Tea was brewed twice a day, the water heated in an old copper urn, and taken round to everyone on a tray.

The clay used in the Pottery was no longer the red clay dug from the site as it had been in Collard's time.   The clay was a standard earthenware body, a mixture of ball and china clay, purchased from Harrisons of Stoke on Trent The arrival of the clay was a problem in the 1960's when there was no polythene, no access to the top of the pottery site and no motorway for the convenience of the lorry driver.   The clay was loaded in lumps, each about 25 kilos, on to cloths on the metal floor of a flat backed lorry.   A load of clay was 10 or more tons. The 200 miles was a full day's journey which shook the clay into a solid lump nearly three feet thick, over the whole area.   It was waiting for us to unload first thing the next day.   This was bad enough in summer but in winter, having been left on the lorry overnight, it was often crusty frozen and difficult to cut out with a spade.

The only entrance to the Pottery at that time was the narrow entrance between no. 30 and no. 32 High Street, about 8 feet 6 inches wide.   The lorry had considerable difficulty turning to back up

and frequently was breathtakingly near knocking down the houses opposite. Later, when articulated lorries were used for this task, it was even more alarming.

Arthur Long was usually on the lorry and the other men, Dave Hickmott, Peter Costa, Ray Boyland, Cyril loving, Alf Johnson, Charlie Pye and others at various times, all put sacks on their shoulders, loaded on a large lump of clay, and staggered up the drive then a flight of steps and up a further slope to the clay store at the top of the site.   In all it was like taking the clay up to the third floor of a house.   It was hard work and took several hours.   It was only possible to use a truck or handcart after we purchased No 30. and could then take the clay up the garden path where there were no steps.

This was a great contrast to the 1980's when we had 20 tons at a time about every four weeks, neatly wrapped in, the now available, polythene bags on a tipper lorry.   This backed up to the top of the pottery and with ease slid its load by the door ready for use. In the early 1960's at the far end of the pottery, in a little lean-to shed, was the casting area. It contained a blunger and several casting racks.   This adjoined the main upper workshop where there were the fettlers, a large drying rack and the Jolly area with its drying cupboard.

Finally in this workshop there was the Glaze spraying area with two dust extractor hoods.
Then there was a flight of stairs leading down to the kiln area.   In the area beyond the kilns there were three working rooms and the warehouses for the finished pots.
Centrally was the main painting room, a small painting room and the mould making room. Plaster moulds were made here for casting and the Jolly machine and had to be carried upstairs to the far end of the pottery!

The lavatories were outside.   A small block with one loo for the men and one for the women. These had only a cold water supply to the block and in winter it was very cold.   I recall on many

occasions the pipes having to be unfrozen with a blow lamp to get any water supply to it.   Needless to say staff did not stay in there very long!   It was not until the new kiln area was built in 1974 that inside facilities were eventually available for the staff.

Harrisons produced a cream matt glaze in bulk for the "Traditional Designs", as approved by the Hulls, as a replacement for the Collard glazes.   As there had been a change to a commercial clay the old glazes would not have the correct expansion and so would not 'fit' the new clay.   This matt glaze was a very stable consistent surface on which to paint and it overcame the risk some of the colours running.

The designs painted on the pots were all based on Collard Jacobean and Persian patterns.
  Several painters from his era were still employed, especially Jessie Bambury and Florrie Richards.

  When we arrived there were paintresses in all three areas all busily working and producing a wide range of Traditional items. The warehouse was already well stocked with several thousand pots. However there were no orders for any of them.   Bill Crane, the full time salesman, had left in

September.   John Levers, his replacement, was not due to start until the 1st. January 1961.   Thus no orders were taken for three months.   John set off on a trip round Cornwall and Devon to existing customers to get their requirements for the summer.   Most did not want anything until Easter.   It was then off to the Blackpool Gift Fair at the end of January.   We had room 216 in the Imperial Hotel.   The whole hotel was reserved for the British Pottery industry's displays.

Our stand, designed by Mr. Chapplow, was stored in Blackpool and erected by a contractor to save us bringing it from Devon each year.   The shelves were painted dark maroon and the walls were hung with dark maroon curtains which made an impressive display as a foil for the pale cream pottery.   .

We then waited, our order books at the ready, for customers.   The only view buyers could see of our products was if they peered round the hotel bedroom door.   Many just looked up at the sign above the door and walked by saying " We don't stock Honiton" Although we did get some orders we were asked for the new designs. They had seen and bought this range last year and wanted new things to put in their shops, Oh, dear! We returned to the pottery with some orders but not nearly enough to cope with the vast stock on our shelves.   There was nothing to be done except drastically reduce the number of staff, especially the paintresses.   It is always a difficult decision to reduce staff because it is they who generate the business for the company.   It had to be done.

The next thing was to decide on what we should make that was new.   We modelled new shapes for the traditional designs but although it was a help it was not "a new range" for the shops to display.   Studio pottery, made by individual craft potters, was much more expensive than commercial factory products.   I decided to try to design ranges of pots which we could make with our commercial techniques but had the feel of studio craft pottery.
We made the Jennifer range consisting of large and small cruets, egg cups, mugs and dishes.   We cast the pieces and scratched a simple pattern with a piece of hacksaw blade, as studio potters do, and then painted on underglaze colours to emphasise the scratch marks.   They then had a transparent gloss glaze applied.

From the Jennifer Range we developed a range of large lamp bases for a lampshade manufacturer, Crookston Royal, in Royston, Herts.   Their local Sales Director, Jim Browning, worked with us on the basic shapes. They were 10" to 18" tall with the centre part scratched and painted with bright underglaze colours.   They ordered them in lots of 200, 300 or even 500 at a time.   The lamps were so large that only a few would fit into a cardboard carton.   We arranged with the local railway station to

provide small wheeled freight containers. These were about 6 ft. by 5 ft by 3 ft. It was an excellent solution to the problem. The orders for the range kept coming for several years.

We sold a quantity of the Jennifer Range but not enough set the world on fire. At the time almost anything new would sell to some of the gift shops. We decided we should make some form of tableware as coffee sets seemed to be the vogue.

We created our Craftsman range which developed over the years and was the Pottery's best seller. To avoid the range looking like a Stoke design we slip cast the cups in a shape which could not be made by machine so that it had a studio image. Initially, we made casseroles by Michael Caddy, a well known designer at the time, from the Royal College of Art, but they were too strange for public taste. We introduced casseroles of our own design to co-ordinate with our craftsman cups. We took the first samples to the Blackpool Gift Fair in several boxes. The car was heavily loaded and we even had a roof rack laden with show samples. It was a long drive, there were no motorways or bypasses, we had to drive through all the towns. It took about 10 hours to complete. When we eventually arrived and unloaded we discovered one important box of Craftsman samples had fallen off! They were never found and we hope they did not cause an accident. The remaining samples were well received. The Craftsman range was our salvation. It not only sold as tableware but the basic blank shapes were used for souvenirs and were decorated in many ways.

I did not like the term 'Art' in the Pottery title " The Honiton Art Potteries Limited", which did not seem to reflect our new developments. There was only one Pottery in Honiton so we changed the name to simply "Honiton Pottery Limited".

While all this was going on there were developments on the Pottery site. No. 30 High Street was purchased in 1963. This allowed us to make great changes and improvements.

The ground floor was opened up and made into a shop/showroom with the office in one corner and other offices and storerooms upstairs. We knocked down the garden wall to give us better access to the back of the house and thus the shop and office. The garage was converted into the packing area store.

We decided we needed still more design expertise so we employed Michael Emmet, a studio potter who was teaching at that time. He was an expert thrower and made large pieces so the old showroom became a throwing and design area for him.

He made the masters moulds for the Woodbury range by hand throwing them. We then cast the pieces in plaster and produced moulds for our slip casting production.

We tried to obtain contract production work and were pleased to meet up with Elaine Goddard, an expert flower arranger who considered she was better than, the then well known, Constance Spry. The Pottery she was working with could not produce the quality and quantity she needed. We made her classic footed, fluted pedestal containers which were all the fashion in House and Garden homes. Some were very small for miniature arrangements.

We continued to trek to the Blackpool Trade Fair, a major event every February, so our exploits were numerous.

We set off about seven in the morning and drove through the towns as there were no motorways or bypasses: Shepton Mallet, Bath and the Fosse Way to try to get to Tewkesbury by mid day. It was then on again through Wolverhampton, Wigan, Warrington, when all the factories were turning out and we reached Blackpool, if lucky,

by about seven in the evening. It took about twice as long as using the motorways although there were very few cars on the road in those days.

There was usually plenty of snow and we always took chains for the tyres. One year the snow was particularly bad,1963, the journey took thirteen hours but without great incident. However on the return journey, we expected conditions to get easier as we travelled further south. When we were almost home we had a problem on sheet ice getting up Hembury Fort Hill, just outside Honiton. In those days the roads were not gritted and salted, one simply drove in the ruts, skidded or got stuck in the ditch. It was out with the shovel to get us home!

We stayed where our predecessors had stayed at the Atlantic Hotel on the Prom. It was a small friendly private hotel. I think our predecessors must have paid their bill in Honiton Pottery because they had one of the best displays I had seen and I am sure the hoteliers were not the buying types! The winters were bitterly cold and the hotel's central heating was minimal. The old sash windows rattled and the wind was so strong that we placed towels on the central gap to stop the draught. The wind picked the towels up!

The Pottery section moved out of the Imperial Hotel in the mid 1960's to the Talbot Hall in the centre of the town. This "Hall" was the main multi-storey car park in Blackpool. Stands consisting of three plain painted walls and a signboard were put up in the car spaces. As you can imagine, there was no heating in a car park. A few, rather dangerous, flame throwing burners were installed .

Edward Du Cann, our local MP, and his wife opened the 17th International Gift Fair in Blackpool in February 1966. They are pictured on our stand in the Talbot Hall looking at our new Craftsman Range of oven-to-tableware. Sales at Blackpool did improve for us because our products could be seen by all passers-by and we had different products on show. This site did not last for many years because eventually the International Gift Fair moved to the brand new National Exhibition Centre in Birmingham.

Our sales pattern developed over the 1960's. It began the year with a Stockroom in an hotel in Newquay at the beginning of January followed by Blackpool at the beginning of February. During the Spring our representative toured around to obtain orders and in July we went to the Harrogate Gift Fair to procure orders for the Christmas season. We appointed various commission sales agents who to cover other parts of the country and they helped on our Show stands.

In 1965 Wolford Chapel, near Honiton, was given to the people of Canada. This was because it was the family Chapel of the Simcoe family. Lieutenant General John Graves Simcoe was the First Lieutenant Governor of Upper Canada (Ontario). There was an obvious chance for us to make a souvenir!

I had the opportunity to go with a sales mission of British Potters to the British Trade Centre in Toronto. We sold the souvenir plates to several department stores and also some of our table-ware.

Philip Cowell, the Chairman of the company, was living in Canada, and with an obvious interest in pottery production, found details of a new Ram Press machine in America. We discussed it and it seemed ideal for our Pottery. We decided to make the investment in it in 1968 This was possibly the most important manufacturing development in all our years at the pottery. It nearly brought us to our knees but once it was up and running it was an outstanding success and all thanks to Philip Cowell's foresight. Several of the Stoke potteries, Wedgwood, Doulton, Crown Derby and others had been to see it in America but had not purchased. They, with the usual Stoke attitude, said no one could tell them how to make pots, they were the world experts! There were lots of legal documents to sign as the whole process was governed by several patents. I flew to Springfield, Ohio for a two week course on mould making and machine operation. Having learned the technique, I made a mould for our oval plate and learned how to operate a press I had to bring back with me, on the plane, the master pattern of holes for the location of the metal mould rings. This would enable us to make the moulds in England. The pattern was a piece of steel almost 2 feet long 3 inches wide and 1 inch thick. It weighed about 12 pounds, far more than I should haven taken in the cabin. I tried to look casual, not declaring it, as I checked in with it wrapped in newspaper under my arm.

On my return I went to British Gypsum to buy the special 'alpha' plaster for the moulds although they did not have any but they said they could make some.

In order to accommodate the Press we had to move the casting area into the main making area, dispense with the Jolly and knock down the Jolly mould drying store. We re-aligned the hot water pipes heating it and then removed the spraying area downstairs to the old packing area. Moving the spraying area saved us carrying every piece of pottery back upstairs after firing and then back down again.

We had the press delivered and we had a special 60 ft. dryer made to fit along the top building. The press was capable of making anything between 800 and 4000 pots a day so we needed this conveyor belt dryer to take the pots away from the machine to be fettled. What a difference it made! It was not without its teething troubles but ultimately wonderful. Our plaster problem was eventually solved by buying a special type from Germany. Ram had sold a press to Germany and their plaster supplier had made an excellent match for the US one. The mould I made in Ohio was for an oval dinner plate which was shipped with the press.

There were many advantages with the machine. When we made small items like our 4" square souvenir dishes we had a mould with 4 cavities so 1000 pressings made 4000 dishes. Inevitably we did not need quite so many of an item at one time so changed the moulds during the day to meet the sales needs. A change over would take about half an hour.

At one time we were the only Pottery in the UK to have a Ram Press. There was only one other in the whole of Europe and that was the German one. Once we had it working properly it was very efficient so we negotiated to be the Ram Press Sales Agent for the UK.

We demonstrated it to Wedgwood; Royal Doulton, who bought two presses; Henry Watson, who bought one; Crown Derby, who bought one; and other major Potteries. The first presses came from America but then we arranged to have them made at Shands in Axminster. At that time there was no other way of making non-round pottery shapes efficiently. In fact Crown Derby were about a year behind their order book for their fluted edge dinner and side plates which took their skilled potter about 15 minutes each to make. They gave us a model. We made a mould and they came to visit us with their special bone china clay. We made about 30 plates in 15 minutes so we had an order straight away and very soon after the press was delivered they were up-to-date with their orders. Henry Watson's Pottery made Terracotta Chicken Bricks for cooking and had orders far in excess of their production capability so we supplied them with a press. I don't know how many thousands it made but it was still producing them more then thirty years later in 2002.

The Ram Press made our Craftsman range of shapes, plates, baking dishes and flan dishes which were an on-going success. We originally made the range in a mottled blue but it was difficult to control the colour. We were noted for our Traditional matt glaze and had the expertise in spraying matt glaze so we made the Craftsman range in matt brown and a burnt orange colour, which we appropriately called Devon red. The matt brown was still in production when we eventually sold the pottery twenty five years later. The great successes of the range were the plate shapes, flat with a turned up edge, which were made in oval and round and the shapes of the coffee cups and beakers. All of which were unlike anything made by the mass production potters in Stoke.

The Ram Press enabled us to design and make a very interesting range of pottery for flower displays. In the late 1960s and early 1970s Ikebana arrangements were a new thing. A Party Plan firm called Flower Beauty developed a plastic pin holder to support these flower displays. This company started in the USA and we manufactured pottery for their British sales team Our specially designed shell shapes and flatish dishes with flutes were considered perfect for promoting their pinholders. The use of our pots with their pinholders was demonstrated and was a great sales success. It inspired housewives, with little or no flower arranging knowledge, to create dramatic displays impressing friends and really beatifying their homes.

In January1967 the Blackpool Gift Fair organisers started a new Gift Fair in Torquay. It was a great success for us especially for the first few years. We took many thousands of pounds of orders for our Craftsman range. The Palace Hotel was the venue and we had our stand on their indoor tennis court. It was a good place but, like the Talbot Hall in Blackpool, it had no proper heating. Later in the day, as the place warmed up, the condensation on the glass roof started pouring water onto us and the customers. It was just one of the many pleasures of Trade Shows!

Thinking that we should concentrate on special designs we worked hard to develop our souvenir range. Firstly we commissioned David Harris a local graphic designer to draw some local scenes and had them made into transfers.

We also developed a technique for screen printing which we used on many thousands of pieces. It was ideal for souvenir dishes and the range of hand coloured dishes of owls, fish hedgehogs etc. designed by Julian Roebuck. We had some particular projects and some good orders for dishes and bowls for events such as Mayflower 1970, the Pilgrim Father's Voyage to America. We produced a signed limited edition of large bowls, all of which sold very quickly, and also large oval platters. Half the production went to Fort Lauderdale in the USA. Our sales agent for Southern England, Harry Cutler, took one of the large Mayflower Dishes to the Bournemouth Gift Fair, yet another Gift Trade Show, and it won the "Best Product of the Show" Award.

The Mayor of Honiton, Councillor Reg. Thomas, was presented with a Mayflower Plate. Jennie, with her great public spirit for duty, had become a Town Councillor for the St Paul's Ward of Honiton in 1967.

The Royal Wedding of Prince Charles and Lady Diana was memorable at the Pottery for several reasons. We produced many special souvenirs for the occasion which was important and very interesting for us. We negotiated with the press in Fleet Street to have the right to produce photo-

graphs on the plate. We think we made some of the most tasteful and attractive designs for the event

Apart from the commemorative 'potties' made for the Bristol 'Chamber' of Commerce. The picture shows our staff enjoying the joke.

As everyone recalls it was a public holiday. Our wake-up alarm was set later than usual and the plan was to watch the event on television. We, with everyone else, looked forward to the day off. Our wake-up call was earlier than expected and from the Fire Service to say that the Pottery was on fire! The residents in the flats overlooking the site had heard cracks and bangs which they found came from the burning roof of the kiln area and not from early morning celebratory fireworks The wooden roof beams, tinder dry by being more than forty years above the kilns, had caught alight. The simple corrugated type roof was ruined but luckily the fire caused no other damage, thanks to our efficient local Brigade. The kilns themselves, designed for heat, were not affected. Perryman Bros., a local building firm, came to the rescue and covered the hole in the roof with a tarpaulin. It was a minor insurance claim but an eventful start to a Public Holiday.

From the beginning of the late 1960s and through the 1970s there were great changes in the South West. Previously, when the major national factories closed for their two week annual holiday, the workers descended by train, en masse, to British resorts. Originally not everyone went away every year, so holiday gifts by the thousand were taken back to the family and friends. Holiday makers saw things not available in their local shops. Then cars became more numerous, cheaper air flights were starting and holiday patterns changed. The West Country holiday industry began to decline because of the vogue for cheap holidays to Spain in the sun .

The potty polishers

The country came out of a recession and a major house building programme began. It gave the interior decorating and house furnishing market huge sales potential.

There was a need for Gift Fairs in the early summer for the shops to stock up for the Christmas trade. We did not usually exhibit at the London shows but always had stands at the Harrogate Gift Fair. Not only was Harrogate a good show for business but it was a pleasant place to spend a week on business! We sometimes stayed in an hotel and at other times took our caravan. We were always heavily laden with the shelves, stands and pots.

During the summers, in particular, we had ever increasing numbers of visitors as we developed the Pottery as a visitor attraction. They had free parking and a walk-round tour. They were a life line for selling our seconds in the shop. The details of our making methods are noted in another chapter of this book. We had an activity area for visitors to 'paint a pot' for themselves and an area for 'throwing' pots. Both our children, Jacqueline and Simon, helped here in their school holidays.

In 1974 we managed to purchase Mont-pellier, No. 32 High Street. This dou-bled our flourishing retail sales space on the site. However it was difficult because the driveway divided our two shops. The driveway could not be closed because No. 34 High Street had a right of way to their garage and a rear entrance. It was not until we were able to purchase No. 34 that we could eventually link the shops. That was in November 1979. We had bought the allotment area behind Nos. 20 to 28 and entrance between Nos. 18 and 20 High Street to give us vehicle access to the pottery, in June 1976. It also gave us parking space for cars and coaches.

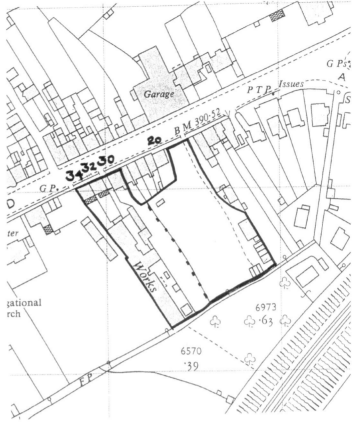

For the Queen's Silver Jubilee in 1977, as with most potteries, we made a range of special souvenirs. It was designed by Julian Roebuck and was a "firework sym-bol". The transfer was not actually in sil-ver because on pottery it is not stable so we had it printed in platinum, which looked silver and maintains its brilliance. Most of the schools on East Devon bought our mugs to present to the children and we sold dishes and mugs not only in our shop but to other out-lets.

Julie Galuszka (Cummins), our designer straight from College, had made some fun egg cups in the form of cars and planes which we were able to produce on the Ram Press. We took them to the Birmingham Spring Fair in 1978 and they were an instant success. We sold thousands of them to our home customers and to many people abroad.

1980 was an important year for the production development with the installation of the Pad Printing machine. It was needed in the painting room but was too large to go through any of the doors.

Again with Perryman's help we unloaded it with a borrowed forklift truck. The men took out one of the large painting room windows and knocked the wall beneath it to the ground. There was still not enough space for the machine and the fork lift to enter so with rollers and timber levers we inched it into the room. The wall was rebuilt and the window replaced and we were in production.

(This, I am reminded by my wife, was an interesting way to celebrate our 20th, china, wedding anniversary!)

Details of the production technique is in the Works Tour section. An illustration is included showing clocks being printed. We printed the decoration of all our Royal Wedding and other souvenirs by this method.

We built an extension to the top pottery area and installed a new 3 cubic metre electric trolley hearth kiln adjoining the fettling area. This avoided having to carry all of the pots down stairs for biscuit firing.

The Ram Press produced more than 1000 items a day. These, added to the slip cast production, were swamping our busy hand sprayers. We desperately needed more spraying capacity so bought a semi-automatic spraying machine which we installed alongside the new kiln.

When we built this extension we installed a large deep settlement pit built into the floor of the new kiln area. This was to prevent our waste clay being washed down the drains and perhaps clogging the town's main sewer. The pit was about 10 feet long, 3 feet wide and sloped from 4 feet to 10 feet deep with five baffle boards acting as dams to slow the water flow. All the casters and fettlers waste water drained into it. It had special chemical blocks added to make the clay settle. The smelly sludge was frequently pumped out. Every month an inspector from South West Water would come with his little bottle and take water samples from our drains to be analysed for solids and any nasty chemical we discharged. Only once or twice did we have to pay a small extra charge because we had been naughty!

A few years later we extended the Pottery again to accommodate the Service Mug making machine which we bought from Devonmoor Pottery. How we made the mugs are detailed in the production chapter. At this time there seemed to be plenty of orders and we were even buying thousands of mugs from John Tams in Stoke. Their mugs were very basic white and much cheaper than we could make. We still needed to make, on the mugs machine, our own unique mug shapes, as well as cups, sugar bowls and other items. The use of the mug machine made our products competitive.

In December 1979, as our electricity demand increased, the South West Electricity Boards put a sub station on our site not only to supply us but also to supply the expanding town of Honiton. In 1980 we were commissioned to make the Exeter 1900th Anniversary souvenirs. Julian Roebuck designed the logo which was put on plates, mugs and dishes. They were sold in the shops and presented to many Dignitaries visiting the City.

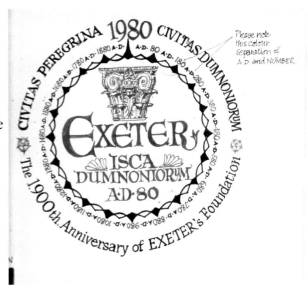

Searching through the history of Pottery in the town we thought at that time that the earliest known pottery on our site was 1881. In 1981 we had just joined the shops together by building in the old driveway. The blank wall on the High Street needed decorating so we created a small tile panel with the date. We also painted a large tile panel in Traditional Jacobean pattern. Alison Wilmington drew out the design and she, with the painters, worked on it. All the other pottery staff, fettlers, kiln loaders, sprayers glaze mixers and the shop staff all painted a little bit. We hope it is an historic reminder of the people who worked for us at the time. The Honiton Museum has a chart of the design and name of those who painted the various parts.

We made souvenirs for the Honiton Museum with a picture of a Honiton lace maker.

Each year a feature in the town is the Honiton Show, a one day agricultural event in August. As we were one of the main traders in the town we always had stand in the Honiton Chamber of Commerce Trade tent. It was hours of work preparing a load of "Special Bargains". The farmers always liked bargains! We took stands, sign boards, flower displays (by Jennie), and enough pots to sell and still have a attractive display left at the end of the day. It required several car loads. It was quite fun meeting the people of the area who were enjoying the sunny day or perhaps the pouring rain.

While all this was going on, we made vast quantities of pottery for a Len Younger who ran a party plan in Bournemouth and traded as Wessex Pottery. His business lasted for several years, then along came Paul Turner who traded as "Carla Pottery". He operated from Bristol and developed a very large Party Plan operation with, I believe, about forty girls selling for him. We made our Craftsman shapes with a special glossy cream glaze with a lily transfer. We also made house name plates and other items for him. He made a very good video of our production, a DVD copy is in the Honiton Museum.

At the same time we made large quantities of ceramic clock faces. Jennie was on our Trade stand at the Olympia Gift Fair and a chap came on to the stand and asked "Can you make half a tea pot?" Jennie thought .. Which half? A few 'hums' and 'ares' later it transpired that he wanted them as kitchen wall clocks. Our Ram Press was ideal for the clay production and our pad printer dealt with the printing of the clock faces. We made many hundreds in white and various colours including bright red enamel.

We exhibited at the Frankfurt Gift Fair every Spring and Autumn, for several years, as part of the British Pottery Manufacturers Federation group. We had a small stand in a back aisle on the third floor. We did sell a lot of our Jane Willingale hand painted ware to the buyer for Bloomingdales of New York. However the contact which was most helpful there was with Cuthbertsons. They were, and perhaps still are, a major supplier of Christmas Pottery in the United States. They were buying from Burgess and Lee of Stoke and Prinknash Pottery both of which companies were exhibiting beside us. Our aisle of exhibitors all met up after the Fair closed for the night and had drinks and meals together. It transpired that Cuthbertsons were unable to get enough oval, rectangular and tree shaped dishes from those Potteries. Cuthbertsons' buyer visited our stand having joined us the previous evening. We showed him ours and he placed orders for thousands of each shape. We supplied them for about six years until they eventually bought all their range from China. The Far East was the dilemma of the whole of the British Pottery Industry.

In 1984 our retail Shop on the High Street was doing well but was now almost too big as it covered the whole ground floor area of three houses and the old driveway. It was more than 100 feet long. We decided to open a Coffee Corner which was more of a 'snug' than a restaurant. Many people used it and we had a regular local trade.

We advertised the Pottery and Shop many times in the year in the local press and we took a few slots on Devon Air Radio and local TV featuring West Country holiday activities. We became a regular stop for coach parties.

Mrs Nora Cowell, the Chairman's wife was a very good artist who had studied extensively when she lived in Toronto. On her retirement to Broadhembury, for fun, she opened an Art Shop in New Street Honiton, called Hobby Horse, selling artists materials. It was a very merry meeting place for her friends and local artists.

Honiton Pottery Shop
Coffee Corner

Cup of Coffee	70p
Mug of Coffee	80p
Pot of Tea, 1 person	60p
Pot of Tea, 2 person	£1.10
Special Teas	60p
Hot Chocolate	70p
Coke	50p
Squash	35p
Orange Juice	60p
Milk	40p
Milk Shakes, super	£1.30

Vanilla Ice Cream with choc. or strawb. sauce 95p

Devon Cream Tea £2.95

After a few years she really did almost retire because we had space in which we could incorporate the Hobby Horse in our Pottery shop.

Our local MPs such as Gwyneth Dunwoody and Peter Emery visited the Pottery and Shop perhaps as much for their benefit as ours, but it was always welcome publicity. We had a major feature about the Pottery in Devon Life in 1986 and a feature of our Loudware designed by Jane Willingale in the Independent in 1989.

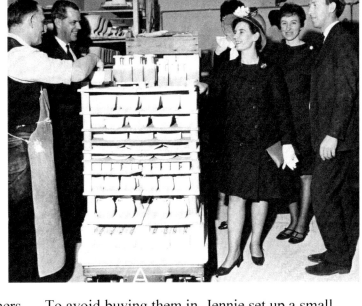

Because we made pottery lamp bases we needed lampshades We required them for both the shop and for our trade customers. To avoid buying them in, Jennie set up a small lampshade manufacturing unit upstairs above the shop where we installed a cutting room and a 'mutual' shade making machine. Jennie's mathematical expertise was well used calculating the size and shape of the various truncated cones for the conical lampshades we required. Jean Gigg, Peter Costa's daughter, was the chief maker. We had many rolls of a variety of fabrics laminated commercially on to card or plastic. I think at this time we were the main shop supplying lampshades in the town. We made many shades to order using customers own fabric which we individually laminated for them. Hessian was very fashionable at the time for shades and wall coverings. Philip Cowell had a contact with an Indian hessian manufacturer so we set up an importing company called Mautostar Ltd. for practical reasons to be independent of the Pottery. We bought dozens of rolls in a variety of colours. We sold hundreds of lamps to Boots with hessian shades for their lighting departments.

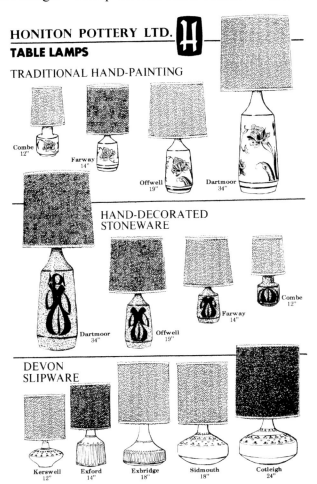

Our search for new orders with the major retailers continued but without much success. We could not break into John Lewis, British Home Stores or Habitat, not for the want of trying. They had set up buying offices on the continent mainly in Italy and Spain. This was to cover their gift requirements of their china and lighting departments. It seemed that in order to justify their overseas office they could not buy from us. We did manage orders from Harrods, Selfridges and Dingles but not in any great volume. The holiday industry was still changing as more people went abroad for their holidays. The West Country gift trade, for pottery, was reducing rapidly.

Our Craftsman range was taken by many coffee shops and restaurants in Exeter, Torquay and other parts of the country.   Pizzaland started with our products for their first few restaurants but as they expanded the big potters in Stoke joined in and we eventually lost out to them. At this time we became involved with Alan Caiger-Smith of Aldermaston Pottery who had cafe and restaurant orders for his hand painted products.   As a craft Pottery, hand throwing most of the pieces, he was unable to produce his products in volume at a reasonable price.   We, with bulk production and as expert hand painters, were able to decorate our oven-to-tableware with his designs under licence.   The design was painted with a wide flat sable brush and the colour was a mixture of cobalt oxide with a little copper oxide added. The copper broke the strong blue colour and gave it a delicate subtlety.   I thought the range was very attractive.

There was always the pub ashtray business in which we were involved. We made some for local pubs but as the cigarette companies supplied free ashtrays, they became our main customers. I can not remember how many thousands of square black ashtrays we made for Rothmans. They were very sophisticated with a deep red and gold transfer.

Whiteways was a substantial local cider manufacturer with their factory at Whimple, a few miles from Honiton, until it was taken over by Showerings. We made pottery barrels for pubs to use to promote their cider sales.   We made them to hold about a gallon and to resemble the old wooden casks. They were fitted with beech wood taps.

We supplied Shepherd Neame, a pub chain in the South East, with crockery for a considerable number of their pubs with their company logo, .

With the very varied mix of products it was necessary to try to establish a costing system to cope with our pricing needs.   After floundering for some time we worked with one of the lecturers from Bournemouth University, Tony Jay, who came for the day. He scratched his head, used his expertise, and returned a week later with suggestions. This went on for some months and he developed a scheme which we could put on our Amstrad computer with 20k memory! We weighed the pot for clay used, measured the pot for kiln sizing and firing costs, how may firings would it need, glazing time and glaze used, painting or transferring, gold edge and packing and despatch costs.   Like magic we had an answer.   Then we at least doubled it!   Anyway we had something to base our costs on if not a selling price.

We were members of the British Pottery Manufacturers Federation in Stoke on Trent for many years.   They were useful to us supplying information about developments in the industry.   They always circularised enquiries from people wanting bulk quantities of pottery and a few wanting their own special designs made. We followed up any that seemed hopeful.   One was from Maryse Boxer wanting her special design of tableware.   After a telephone call Jennie and I set off to London to meet her at her flat in Cadogan Square.   She was there with her husband, in a very sophisticated and stylish apartment.   Her very innovative ideas included totally flat square, rectangular and lotus shape plates. If you recall this was completely unheard of in the early 1980's. Since 2000 most of the fashion conscious restaurants, hotels and cafes use unconventional non-round shaped tableware.   It was Maryse Boxer who started the trend. Of all the hundreds of potteries in the Federation we were the only one to respond to her enquiry. We managed to point out that the gravy or a sauce would just pour off a completely flat surface so she accepted Jennie's suggestion of a slightly upturned edge. It was a range that was perfect for our production, in quantity, on our Ram Press. Barry Ward made an excellent job of modelling the shapes and the whole project was a great success..

The items were originally produced in black or white which had a very dramatic effect. A lotus shape plate with the food on it was placed on a contrasting colour square plate. The colours were alternated around the table. The range developed with smaller square and rectangular shapes, then bowls were added. Coloured glazes were used and some pieces had gold banding. The Boxers did their own marketing at Trade Shows here and overseas and they had orders not only from department and specialist stores here but also from the US, France, Japan and Australia. They became a very major customer of the Pottery. Her designs of our plates etc., were included in the Victoria and Albert Museum's feature of special 20th century ceramics.

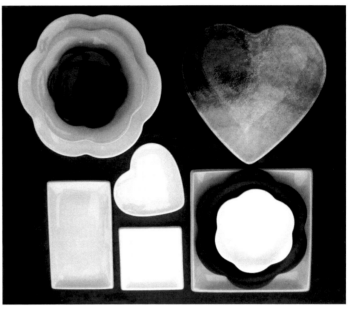

We had several interesting special projects like the one for Harvey Nichols in Knightsbridge. They commissioned designs of odd animals and birds to promote the various departments. Large models were made for the window displays and we made pottery decorated to match.

One of the last quite major customised orders we had was for the start up of the Old Shanghai Restaurant in Brighton. Hundreds of plates and dishes were decorated with a Chinese warrior. They paid us a small amount initially. We delivered the goods to the splendid establishment and we could not get our payment. There was obviously a problem. There was a meeting of all the people who were owed money, builders, decorators, kitchen equipment suppliers and ourselves. Our pottery was not a fixture so I hired a van and drove to Brighton. In some trepidation I demanded our pottery back. I think they were so surprised they helped me load it. I drove it away. We were able to reglaze it and sell most of it in our shop. It was an expensive lesson!

For some reason we became very interested in Post boxes. Jennie joined the Letter Box Society and we made a range of Post Box money boxes. Apart from the standard cylindrical red box we made a version of the Victorian Penfold shape which we produced in the original dark green colour as well as red. The Channel Island of Guernsey have their boxes in blue so we made specials for them. We tried to sell them in bulk to the Post Office head quarters, but only tried a few. Harrods and many gift shops sold them.

It became obvious in the late 1980's that the

Pottery could not get sufficient orders to sustain the forty people on the payroll.   We tried many avenues to get substantial orders from major customers.   Little did we know that the whole Pottery industry in Stoke on Trent was also suffering.

We met up with Mr Samuel Heath, a metal ware manufacturer, who also owned Dartmouth Pottery, at the Birmingham Trade Fair.   We asked him if he was interested in forming some kind of joint venture.   Unknown to us at the time, the UK agent for Cuthbertsons Christmas Tree Company was acting as a pottery consultant advising Samuel Heath.   I subsequently discovered that he had told them to either expand or to close Dartmouth Pottery.

The outcome of our discussions was the sale of all of our pottery equipment, moulds, designs and orders to Dartmouth in November 1991.   We were specialists in hand painting but Dartmouth did not have this skill, so we retained the hand painted designs to produce and sell in our shop. We retained the few trade customers wanting them.   We sold the name of "Honiton Pottery" to them but retained the name of "The Honiton Pottery Shop".   The major customer we handed over was Maryse Boxer.

It was sad to see it all go but a reasonable solution for us.   The potters all departed with sadness and were paid their redundancy.   We sold the main Pottery site in 1992 as a building site for housing which they thoughtfully called "Pottery Close".

The Pottery buildings were pulled down.   We were left with our factory stock, thousands of pots, which Dartmouth, understandably, did not want.   There were many too many to put in the shop so we piled them in our car park covered with tarpaulins.   We had the three houses nos. 30, 32 and 34 which comprised the shop.   Without the hundreds of visitors, frequently in coach loads, coming to look round the pottery, the retail space was much too large.   In 1994 we sold Nos. 32 and 34 to East Devon District Council to develop as a venue for "Mind".

We still had some trade customers so we decided we needed a trading name because retailers would not buy from a retail shop.   We therefore launched "Signature of Honiton" to sell our products to other shops.

We kept Caroline Wright, one of our very skilled painters and decorators and Barry Ward, our mould maker.   Caroline continued to hand paint designs of Roses, Tropical and Poppy for the shop and transfer decorate many of the blank items.   We made back stamps for them saying "Honiton Pottery Shop".

We wanted to make more customised items to go with our personalised Commemorative and House name plates.   Barry, using the resin technology from pottery mould making and his skill as a modeller, made moulds for our resin items and cast them for us.   We could offer fridge magnet letter boxes and a range of letter openers with special handles, Graduates in gowns, Post boxes and particular people. These we hand painted and engraved with names on the blades using the sandblasting machine which we bought. We could also use this to engrave special designs on glass further extending our customised product range.

A rather special order came from The Bank of England. We modelled their "Gateman" in his uniform and engraved the blades. We made 100 as Christmas gifts for their staff. I hope some are still in use in high places!

Amongst the special items we were delighted to design and to produce a plate for the Honiton Pottery Collectors Society to celebrate their 10th Anniversary.
We were looking forward to our retirement and we arranged to lease the shop to Martin and Christine Wallis at the end of October 1996. After many happy years, with a few anxious moments, we ceased owning and running Honiton Pottery.

A wide selection of Honiton Pottery is now on display at the Honiton Museum.

How we made
HONITON POTTERY

******

A tour of the Pottery
Explaining the processes in each department

******

This is a historic record
Of some of the various techniques used in the pottery industry
Between the 1960's and the 1990's

*****

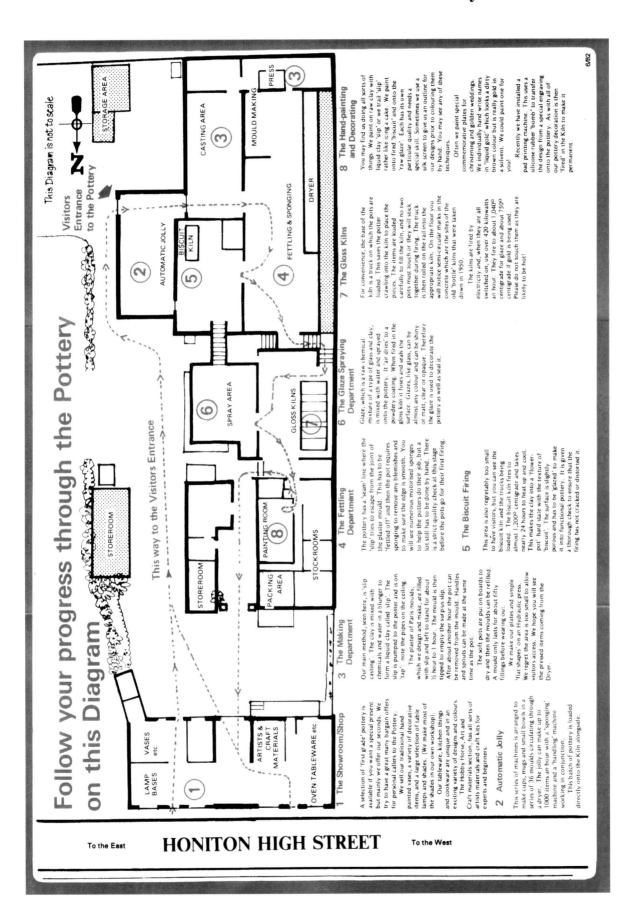

Follow your progress through the Pottery on this Diagram

This Diagram is not to scale

N

Visitors Entrance to the Pottery

This way to the Visitors Entrance

STORAGE AREA — STOREROOM — VASES etc. — LAMP BASES — ARTISTS & CRAFT MATERIALS — OVEN TABLEWARE etc. — CASTING AREA — MOULD MAKING — PRESS — AUTOMATIC JOLLY — BISCUIT KILN — FETTLING & SPONGING — DRYER — SPRAY AREA — GLOSS KILNS — PACKING AREA — PAINTING ROOM — STOCKROOMS — STOREROOM

To the East — **HONITON HIGH STREET** — To the West

6/82

1 The Showroom/Shop

A selection of 'first grade' pottery is available if you want a special present but mainly we offer our seconds. We try to have a great many bargain offers for personal callers to the Pottery.

We sell our traditional hand painted vases, a variety of decorative items, and a large selection of table lamps and shades. (We make most of the shades in our own workshop).

Our tableware, kitchen things and cookware are unique and in an exciting variety of designs and colours. The Hobby Horse, Art and Craft materials section, has all sorts of artists materials and craft kits for experts and beginners.

2 Automatic Jolly

This series of machines is arranged to make cups, mugs and small bowls in a series of 36 moulds circulating through a dryer. The jolly can make up to 1000 items an hour with a 'sponging' machine and a 'handling' machine working in conjunction.

This batch of pottery is loaded directly onto the Kiln alongside.

3 The Making Department

Our main method, seen here, is 'slip casting'. The clay is mixed with chemicals and water in a blunger to form a liquid clay called 'slip'. The slip is pumped to the potter and is on 'tap': note the pipes on the ceiling.

The plaster of Paris moulds, which we design and make, are filled with slip and left to stand for about ½ hour to 1 hour. The mould is then tipped to empty the surplus slip.

After about another hour the pot can be removed from the mould. Handles and spouts can be made at the same time as the pot.

The soft pots are put on boards to dry and then the moulds can be refilled. A mould only lasts for about fifty fillings before wearing out.

We make our plates and simple 'flat shapes' on an Hydraulic press. We regret the area is too small to allow visitors access. We hope you will see the pressed items coming from the Dryer.

4 The Fettling Department

The pottery has a 'seam' line where the 'slip' tries to escape from the joint of the plaster mould. This has to be 'fettled off' and then the pot requires sponging to remove any blemishes and to make sure the edge is smooth. You will see numerous motorised sponges to help the potters do their job, but a lot still has to be done by hand. There is a strict quality check at this stage before the pots go for their first firing.

5 The Biscuit Firing

This area is also regrettably too small to have visitors, but you can see the biscuit kiln and the trucks being loaded. The biscuit kiln fires to almost 1,200° centigrade and takes nearly 24 hours to heat up and cool. This makes the clay into a 'flower-pot' hard state with the texture of 'biscuit'. The surface is slightly porous and has to be 'glazed' to make it into functional pottery. It is given a thorough check to ensure that the firing has not cracked or distorted it.

6 The Glaze Spraying Department

Glaze, which is a raw chemical mixture of a type of glass and clay, is mixed with water and sprayed onto the pottery. It 'air dries' to a powdery coating. When fired in the gloss kiln it fuses and seals the surface. Glazes, like glass, can be almost any colour and can be shiny or matt, clear or opaque. Therefore the glaze is used to decorate the pottery as well as seal it.

7 The Gloss Kilns

For convenience, the base of the kiln is a truck on which the pots are loaded. This saves the potter crawling into the kiln to place the pieces. The items are loaded carefully to fill the kiln, and no two pots must touch or they will stick together during firing. The truck is then rolled on the rail into the appropriate kiln. On the floor you will notice semi-circular marks in the concrete which are the sites of the old 'bottle' kilns that were taken down in 1950.

The kilns are fired by electricity and, when they are all switched on, use over 420 kilowatts an hour. They fire to about 1,040° centigrade for glaze and about 750° centigrade if gold is being used. Please do not touch them as they are likely to be hot!

8 The Hand-painting and Decorating

You may find us doing all sorts of things. We paint on raw clay with liquid clay 'slip' or we trail 'slip' rather like icing a cake. We paint onto fired 'biscuit' and onto the 'raw glaze'. Each has its own particular quality and needs a special skill. Sometimes we use a silk screen to give us an outline for our designs prior to colouring them by hand. You may see any of these techniques.

Often we paint special commemorative plates for christening and golden weddings. We individually hand write names in 'liquid gold' which looks a dirty brown colour but is really gold in a solvent. We could paint one for you!

Recently we have installed a pad printing machine. This uses a silicone rubber 'bomb' to transfer the design from a special engraving onto the pottery. As with all of our pottery decoration is then 'fired' in the Kiln to make it permanent.

The handout shows the layout of the pottery during the 1980's.

Since the time when Charles Collard started at Honiton, visitors were invited to see the pottery being made and admission was 'free' This appealed to families and coach parties alike on those, all too frequent, wet days in summer. They were welcome and made a very important contribution to our retail shop sales.

The clay from the site used by Collard had to be dug, left to weather, sieved and "pugged" to prepare it for use. To avoid this relatively unproductive work the Hulls bought in a ready prepared special earthenware clay mixture. This had the advantage that it was a consistent factory controlled standard made for commercial production and not for hand throwing. I tried throwing with it but it had no "body" to hold up a tall shape, It gently sank down after I stopped working it. In contrast it was ideal for the Jolly because the plaster mould supported it in the required shape and when used for slip casting the chemicals made it flow easily with very little additional water.

Before the use of polythene bags the clay 'lump' was stored in a corrugated iron lean-to shed and was covered with wet cloths and a tarpaulin to keep it moist and in good condition for making. To prevent the clay freezing in the shed in winter, we bought gallons of paraffin from the local ironmonger to use in the rather battered old Valor stoves.

The methods used to form the basic pottery shapes.

The plan of the pottery layout shows the three main clay production areas then in use; slip casting in plaster moulds, Ram pressing which replaced the old 'Jolly' and the mug machine.

Slip Casting. Liquid clay, called 'slip' was poured into Plaster of Paris moulds which absorbed water from the slip to form the pots. To produce the slip, clay was put into the 'Blunger', a 300 gallon metal mixer driven by a 4 horse power motor. A minimum amount of water and chemicals were added to deflocculate the clay, separating the particles and make it 'flow'. The chemicals used were sodium silicate and soda ash, These ensured that the casting process was speedy and the moulds did not have to absorb too much water. The slip needed to be accurately controlled. The aim was to have a pint of free flowing slip weighing exactly 36 ozs, (a pint of water weighs only 22 ozs). An ounce more or less of the chemicals in the 300 gallons was critical and would throw the whole mixture out of balance. The slip then had to be checked on a torsion viscometer which registers the fluidity. It was then left for exactly one minute and tested again to see how much it had 'jelled' If the slip did not flow correctly slight adjustments of the chemicals could be made.

Occasionally if the blunger was filled carelessly the slip would set, the mixing paddles would not turn and it would take most of the day to dig the clay out through the small loading area at the top.   Most of the time it worked well under the expert supervision of Peter Costa.   It was too risky to leave the slip unstirred over weekends and holidays so we would run it for a a few hours every day to ensure that the slip did not set.

The slip came from the blunger into a 120 mesh sieve to remove any lumps, grit or foreign bodies. Eventually this was an electrically powered vibrating sieve.   The slip was then pumped into a 2000 gallon slip arc to stabilise it and for storage.   The arc was a cylindrical fibreglass tank with a slow moving gate paddle rotating at about 20 revs per minute   This kept the slip fluid and allowed any air bubbles to rise out of the slip and avoid serious casting faults.

When needed, the slip was pumped from the slip arc through a pipe system around the ceiling of the casting area.   There were six down-pipes fitted with taps for the casters to use to fill the moulds.

It was not always like that.   Initially in the 1960s the process was simple and unsophisticated.   The same blunger was used and the clay was checked by a hit or miss method and sieved into a bucket.   The bucket was used to fill the big moulds and a jug to fill the small ones.   Unused slip was tipped back into the blunger. That was all the equipment there was.   The pots generally seemed all right but it was very inefficient.   The development to the pumped system was improved over a number of years.   The pipes were initially installed around the roof by our local builder and all the special slip taps and the pump came from Stoke.   Most of the pottery staff came to see this new system switched on.   To the delight of all of us, after a minute or two, slip appeared and we started filling moulds.   Wonderful.   We stood around and were proud of our achievement.   Then suddenly we were showered with the clay slip from the ceiling.   It went everywhere!!!   Unfortunately we had not made a proper return value system. The pressure built up until the pipe work joints gave way and slip rained from the roof. We learnt a lesson.

The making process was to 'fill' a plaster of Paris mould with the clay slip and leave it to stand for about half an hour.   During this time the plaster absorbed water from the clay slip.   The clay in contact with the mould became firm.   As the clay set, less and less water could be absorbed through the solidifying clay into the plaster.   So after 45 minutes the process had almost stopped.   The mould was then 'tipped' so that the remaining liquid slip was

poured out, thus leaving a hollow pot.   If the slip was not a good mixture the pot would be flabby and fall out when the mould was tipped! The slip could have another fault which caused it to form a solid 'gel' which was an equally difficult problem.   The slip would not empty making an almost solid pot.

The pot was then left for about another half an hour, while the inside surface of it dried.   The top was trimmed with a knife by the potter. Trimming was a very important process especially when forming spouts on teapots and the lips of jugs.   Then after a short time, depending on the item, it could be removed from the mould.

The process did not have the romance of hand throwing but had many advantages.   Embossed de-signs and fluting could be incorporated into the mould which opened up extra design potential.   Handles, knobs and spouts for tea pots, jugs and other items were incorporated in the mould.   Being made in one piece they were less vulnerable.

However there are several problems with slip casting which have to be faced.   .As clay dries it shrinks, everyone knows this and it is essential to the potter because it allows the cast pot to release from the mould.   Wonderful! But, as it shrinks it grips tightly round the plaster in the centre of handles which are torn off the pot if it is left in the mould too long.

After being 'filled' about three times moulds have absorbed quite a lot of water and are wet.   In this condition they cast very slowly and so needed drying.   That involved taking them to a heated store and bringing out another set for use. This was heavy physical work and time consuming.   Latterly, but not until the late 1980's did we partially solve the problem by putting big air circulating fans over the casting benches.   These were run all night and dried the moulds quite well.   Otherwise they were put into the heated mould store.   Every pot required its own mould and in order to produce a quantity of pots we had a batch of moulds from 10 to about 50 of each shape.   All of these had to be stored when not in use which took up a great deal of space. Another problem was that a mould could only be used for about 50 filling before it was worn out.

The chemicals that made the clay flow and made the casting process possible, slowly dissolved the surface of the plaster allowing the air holes in the plaster to show.   These caused little bumps on the surface of the pot. As these became more noticeable the 'fettlers' had to sponge away the little bumps as well as the 'seam' lines of the mould joint and the top edge of the pot.   Eventually the moulds had to re-placed.

Mould making was a very skilful full time job and considered so specialised that only a Stoke-on-Trent trained person could be used.   In the 1950s Tom Sherriff, pictured here with a plaster 'case', made the moulds followed by George Hague in the 1960s and then Barry Ansell.   They were all good at their mould making job but did not have a 'craft pottery' feeling when working on new shapes. So we decided to try to train a local person.   Barry Ward proved to be a very fine mould maker and crafts-man.   He worked in great detail and made moulds with great precision. He also modelled almost every shape we made from the 1970s onwards ,including all the very subtle Maryse Boxer designs.

The master shape was made of Plaster of Paris by lathe turning, if round, and other-wise by hand carving. The handles and spouts on all items had to be hand carved.   The solid 'master' shape was marked exactly down the centre line and then set in a clay/plaster bed to the line to make one side of the mould.   The bed was removed and the other side was made.   This mould was called the 'Block' or master mould.   It was dried and then filled with slip to test it.   Assuming it was correct it was not used again for casting to protect the surface. If slight changes were needed they were done and hope-fully only one more test filling was needed.   From this 'block' a 'case' mould was made in a spe-cial strong casting plaster so that production moulds could be made from the 'case'.   The 'blocks' were stored though they may never be needed again.   Because 'case' moulds have a hard working life they were subject to damage on fine details and sometimes the plaster could not stand the stresses and strains.   With the advent of special epoxy resins in the late 1970s we used them for some 'cases', but they were more expensive than plaster.   In the mid 1980s silicone rubbers came on to the market and they were even more expensive.   The material cost of plaster was a few pound but epoxy resins and silicone rubbers were at least ten times more costly.   Now all embossed and detailed master mould are made of epoxy or silicone rubber because of the guaran-teed very high quality.

The Jolly, a type of industrial mechanised potters wheel, was purchased to improve production speeds. It used plaster moulds and metal tools to produce all the plates, cups, saucers, egg cups and soup bowls.   For example to make a plate the mould forms the top profile of the plate and the tool forms the profile of the 'foot' and back.

The skill required to operate the jolly was not available locally so Alf Johnson came from Stoke. Arthur Long took over in the early 1960s and then the skill was passed on to others especially Charlie Pye.

Making on the Jolly was a two stage process.

Firstly a ball of clay was thrown on to the plaster turntable which rotated for a cycle during which the arm came down and spread it into a flat disc.   If the clay ball was not central on the plaster, the clay disc became very eccentric and the centre of the clay disc, with the stresses and strains of being flattened, would not be in the middle causing problems later.

Secondly the disc was removed and thrown, with a flick of the wrists on to the mould on the Jolly head. The disc must be central and the 'flick' ensured that no air was trapped between the clay and the mould.   Air would prevent it forming correctly and feel like a lump.   The mould then rotated at high speed, water was applied and the tool carefully lowered to form the plate.   Just the right amount of water was needed to lubricate the clay for the tool to force it into shape.   A knife was used to trim the excess clay from the edge of the spinning plate.

The unskilled would have the clay flying off or wrapping round the tool.   Just another piece of clay in the reprocessing bin! If the clay disc was misplaced on the plate mould the finished plate would have eccentric strains causing it to 'twist' during firing.

Pieces were left to dry on the mould. This needed to be an even process or, for example, if there was a draught it would dry that side of the plate more than the

other and could cause warping, twisting and cracking of the piece.   Illustrated is the drying store with saucers on their moulds.

Cups, soup bowls and similar deep shapes were made in hollow moulds.   A ball of clay was thrown into the mould and the tool lowered in to form the inside of the piece, a skilful task.

A Jolly could make one or two items a minute and each one required a mould. A batch of moulds and a tool were needed for a production run.   It took about half an hour to exchange the moulds and reset the tool for a new shape.

Every shape had its set of moulds.   We made side plates, cereal bowls, saucers, coffee saucers, tea and coffee cups, plant pots, jam pot covers etc. which was a

mould storage nightmare. For example imagine the storage and drying space needed for 40 dinner plate moulds laid out side by side.

However this was not an ideal production technique for Honiton. To work efficiently a very large dryer would have been needed and a semi-automated jolly would have been better. It was not a realistic proposition with our limited space.

Jollied items are easy to identify by the small dimple showing in the centre made by the metal tool. The Jolly was in use from the early 1950s until 1968.

So, as mentioned, we installed the Ram Press. The special technology of the Ram process was the compressed air system incorporated in the moulds. The two parts of the working mould, an upper and lower part, were made in precision steel rings. They had a cobweb of air-permeable fabric coils mounted in each as in the first illustration. The special plaster was then mixed and poured

in. As the plaster set, compressed air was gradually introduced until it reached 100psi. The air blew through the surface driving out water. The second illustration shows the lower part of a finished mould drying. The two mould parts were aligned and mounted in the press. Clay was inserted and the 60 ton press was closed forming the pot. Excess clay was squeezed out.

Air was applied to the lower mould which released it from that part and the press was opened with the plate sticking to the top mould. When air was applied to the top mould it was released on to a board, as shown in the third illustration, and removed and placed on the dryer. The press was then ready for another piece of clay to be processed.

The British Gypsum plaster failed because the introduction of the compressed air caused the mould to explode rather than become permeable. It was also very brittle and prone to cracking in use.

Not only would the Ram press produce all the items we made on the Jolly, except cups, but it would also make oval plates, square plates, baking dishes, coasters, teapot stands and many, many, more shapes.

Instead of having to make and store dozens of production moulds for each Jolly shape we only had to have one mould for a shape made when we needed it. Having made

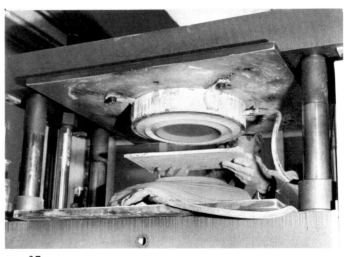

the required number of pots or the mould being worn out the plaster was knocked out of the ring ready to be refilled with the next required shape.

We had conquered the making of plates and cookware on the press.   With "casting" we were able to make the jugs, tea pots and vases but we still did not have a cost effective way to make cups and mugs.   We looked at 'Service' Mug/Cup machines but they were at least £35,000 plus all the tooling and extra ancillary equipment to go alongside them.   Then we discovered the specialist mug makers, Devonmoor Pottery at Bovey Tracey was closing.   They had a Service mug machine for sale including tooling and a handling machine.   We bought it with all the bits and pieces for £10,000.   They made Blue mugs with names on them similar to those in the photograph.

The Mug Machine was installed in a new extension which we built specially beside the top kiln. We had employed John Pennell as assistant manager and that was very helpful because he had come from Stoke and knew how to work the beast of a machine! It could make up to 10 items a minute which gave a potential of nearly 5000 per day, somewhat greater than our needs.   Apart from making the mugs, each one required a handle which had to be cast in slip and trimmed and then stuck on to the mug.   It would have needed an army to process that quantity so we decided on part day running.   We could make tea cups, coffee cups, mugs of various shapes, egg cups, ramekins and a variety of small bowls. As usual there was a learning curve which was soon climbed.

We eventually made the handles on the press, pressing twelve at a time, twice a minute.   We built our own automated handle sponging machine and it was very successful.   The mug machine was an interesting production challenge.   There were 36 moulds in the machine around a big wheel. Each mould in turn was automatically filled with clay, pre-cut to size, and dropped into it.   A rotating metal tool came down and formed the inside of the mug.   The filled mould then went through the drying area of the machine and was removed from the mould by the operator (at ten a minute!).   The mug was then placed on another machine where the top was sponged to ensure the drinking edge was smooth and, while still moist, the handle had to be applied, still at up to ten a minute!   It was an operation which could be done by two people but it was essential to have at least one extra person helping just in case!

We continued to make the named mugs for Devonmoor customers.   It was a declining holiday trade market but still ran into many thousands.   It was sufficient to justify developing a computerised engraving machine to scratch the names.   This machine was especially useful when we had thousands of mugs ordered by a Japanese customer wanting mug with 'Afternoon Tea', 'Morning Cup' and '3 o'clock cup' scratched on them.   The order was repeated for several years which seemed unusual until we found out that there were several cafes called 'Afternoon Tea' in Japan.

The techniques used to finish the clay process prior to firing.

Fettling is the general term used for the process of removing the seam, a ridge where the mould parts come together, and smoothing any blemishes from the surface.

We had a group of fettlers who had to be very versatile because the different clay production methods needed different techniques and skills.

To avoid making very complicated moulds for items such as casseroles, the handles and knobs were made separately.   A special task performed by the fettlers was the sticking on of these knobs and handles. The clay of the pot and the handle had to be 'leather hard'.   The surfaces to be joined had to be roughened and clay 'slip' applied.   The pieces were then pressed together. The slip dissolved part of the two surfaces.   As the clay dried the knob or handle united with the pot to become an integral whole.   It may appear easy in expert hands but if all the conditions were not correct the handle would have fallen off as it dried, or worse, when it was in use.

All items were dried before fettling otherwise the pots could distort easily.   To avoid the potters working in a dusty atmosphere the pottery was 'wet' fettled, that is with a wet sponge.

Fettling the cast items required skill and care to remove the mould seam with a knife without taking chunks out of the pot.   The top had to be levelled and the whole surface lightly sponged.   As technology improved, in the 1970s we commissioned a local retired engineer, Ted Adlam, to make belt sponging machines, as seen in the photograph, before these, the fettler had her hands in and out of a bowl of water, rinsing the sponge, every few seconds.   The machines produced a better product more quickly than having to sponge by hand and it made the job of fettling more pleasant for the staff. The motorised sponge moved at

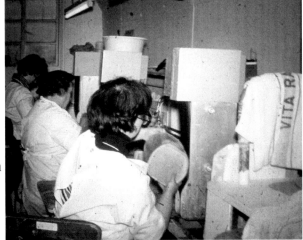

about one foot per second so the pot could be placed against it and without effort is was smoothed.   The sponge passed round the back of the machine through a water bath where it was washed and pressed through rollers to remove excess water.   It reappeared ready to sponge another pot.   This same process was used to fettle all the non round shapes made on the Ram Press.

Round items made on the Press and those made on the Jolly, before we had the Press, were fettled on a 'Towing' wheel.   This was a powered wheel with a vacuum suction running through the centre of the spindle. The wheel 'head' had a shaped top to suit the item being processed. The 'tower' placed the plate on the wheel and the vacuum held the plate while it was spinning. Then with a lump of 'tow', flax (which was used for lagging hot water pipes), in each hand was held against the plate until smooth. This created an enormous amount of dust. The machine had a special dust extractor to avoid choking everyone. Later this was modified to have powered wet sponges to replace the tow and so eliminated the dust problem.

When fettled, all items were thoroughly dried and checked before firing.

In Charles Collard's day the local red clay was fired in the large, coal fired, bottle kiln. It was warmed, with a small fire to ensure everything was dry, on Thursday evening then fired on Friday. It took Saturday and Sunday to cool down ready to be unloaded on Monday. Both biscuit and glazed pots were fired, together, in saggars at the same temperature, about 1,000 degrees Centigrade.

'Saggars' which had been needed to protect the pottery from the coal firing debris, were no longer needed as there was no pollution of the kiln atmosphere from the electricity.

The six trolley hearth kilns in the main kiln area, as mentioned earlier, was sufficient to justify a small electrical substation on the pottery site. The kilns were constructed of low thermal-loss bricks inside a metal casing. The elements were set into grooves along the sides, back, door and in the base of the trolley which formed the kiln floor. As the trolleys were on tram lines they could be loaded, in comfort, outside the kiln. This enabled easy and efficient loading with the maximum number of pots on the truck. The load, when ready for firing, had to be very steady and have the right profile to be wheeled into the kiln.

When fired and cool, the trolley was pulled out and unloaded. There were electric controls setting the speed of firing and automatically switching off each kiln on reaching the required temperature. It all seemed idyllic, which it was, most of the time. The kilns were fired over night, but, if there had been the slightest surge in the power or a storm or any little hiccup to trip off the delicate safety controls, they had to be fired again the next night.

The building was extended upstairs in 1974 to accommodate another kiln due to the increased production from the Ram Press This was purchased from Shelly and was purely for 'biscuit', the first, firing.

The kilns later moved into the 'space age' when Brian Madge started building pottery kilns in Honiton. He was a technical expert and designed them with a ceramic fibre lining. This saved about 25% of the firing cost. We stripped out the inside of all our kilns and installed his special system. Firing was quicker and power was only needed to heat the pots not the brick structure. We also installed new, more sophisticated kiln control equipment.

The Stoke clay needed biscuit firing at a higher temperature (around 1,160 degrees Centigrade) than the glaze firing (around 1,040 degrees Centigrade). The existing Collard glazes would not 'match' the Stoke clay for temperature or thermal expansion. Therefore a new standard matt glaze was developed for the 'Traditional' hand painting that was very consistent but lost some of the romance of the craft pottery produced by Collard. The influence of the industrial pottery industry had come to Honiton.

There was always a production flow problem at the Pottery because of the slope of the ground. Every pot had to be carried down a flight of stairs from the clay making area to the kiln area and sometimes up and down again! The standard pottery technique was to put the pots on 'boards', planks of wood six feet long and one foot wide. These were loaded with twenty jugs or fifty egg cups or thirty plates or what ever and carried by the potters on their shoulders. This they did with very few accidents, round the corners and down the stairs, with great dexterity, strength and skill to the kiln area.

Special methods were needed for loading different items. Plates were fired in piles, called 'bungs', a previously fired plate was used as a 'setter' on the base and about six plates were piled on top. Silver sand was then worked into the sides so that the sand supported the plates, hopefully, to stop them warping and twisting during the firing. To help cups and round items to hold their shapes they had their rims damped with glue and were then placed one on top of the other, rim to rim. Tea pots and other lidded items had their lids on to help the pot and lid keep shape. In this way a biscuit kiln was loaded and put into the kiln for firing.

In commercial earthenware production the biscuit firing was always higher than subsequent firings. This was to stabilise the pottery so that in later firings it did not warp, twist or shrink any more. The shrinkage of clay from wet to the end of the biscuit firing was about ten per cent. The process was not simply to set the kiln to 1,160 degrees Centigrade, it was, as with any cooking, a heat/work process. Although the dials and controls were set, potters also used thermoscope bars and/or Bullers rings inside the kiln. These pieces of special ceramic material were fired with the pottery to record the heat/work. We used Bullers rings scattered around the kiln amongst the pots. If there was an element failure in one part of the kiln, which we detected in the morning, when we checked the kiln, we could re-fire any pots which had not reached the correct temperature. As the kilns fired over night we could not tell when it failed and how much, if any, of the kiln was under-fired except by checking the Bullers rings. Firing was quite an exact science, under-firing could cause 'crazing' and 'chittering' of the glaze while over-firing could cause increased warping and vitrifying of the pot.

Having successfully fired the pots they were then checked for cracks; hitting them with a wooden brush handle to see if they had a clear 'ring'. They were brushed, to remove any sand and checked for blemishes which were repaired. They were then ready for glazing.

In our the early days at the Pottery, before we developed the old packing shed into the spraying area, every pot had to be carried upstairs to be glaze sprayed and back down again for the 'Gloss' firing. The 'Traditional' glaze used from the 1950's did not flow much in firing and therefore it could not be applied by dipping, as Collard had done with his glazes, because the inevitable runs and dribbles would not smooth out during the firing. Thus it was

essential to establish a spray glaze technique at Honiton. The inside of deep items such as jugs, vases etc. were 'rinsed' with a slightly softer glaze, which flowed a little, but all other surfaces were sprayed inside and out. It was a skilful job to get an even coating of glaze around handles and knobs and the underside of items.

We made several attempts to mechanise the spraying and eventually purchased an automatic rotary spray machine. John Pennell was our expert at setting it. This sprayed twelve plates a minute. It had a slowly rotating circular base with six turntables. Plates were put on and as each plate rotated three spray guns tracked across its surface. The guns were adjustable for speed, time and glaze quantity. When operating, plates had to be put on or taken off the turntables with great care.

The raw glaze powder, prepared and supplied by Harrisons of Stoke, was mixed with water so that it weighed 26 oz. to the pint. This kept it thick enough to adhere to the pot. If it was too thin it ran off into a pool at the bottom of the spray hood!

Every pot put into a kiln for the gloss firing had to be supported on a 'stilt', on 'pins' or have the 'foot' wiped clean of glaze. The foot had to be really clean because even the slightest film of glaze could cause the pot to stick to the kiln shelf and pluck a piece out of the foot when the glaze melted during firing. Similarly lids had to be placed separately from their bases so that they did not stick together during gloss firing. Originally we wiped the foot on a piece of tough damp flannel which soon became clogged with glaze and had to be rinsed frequently under a

tap.   We endured this laborious process of rinsing the flannel for many years until we invested in a motorised belt sponger (as illustrated).   This ran the continuous sponge belt through a water bath and then squeezed it through rollers to present a clean working area for wiping the foot of the next pot.   The machine for this simple job cost several hundred pounds and a replacement sponge belt about fifty pounds which was a lot of money in the 1970s.

Trying to create the 'Traditional' Honiton glaze was no easy feat.   It caused Norman Hull and Bill Chapplow many headaches.   I heard stories of Mr. Chapplow throwing pots across the kiln room in desperation and disgust when the glaze failed to get to the standard he required.   An acceptable glaze was obtained in 1959.   The hand painting on the raw glaze, prior to the final glaze firing, was a problem because the raw glaze dried to a dusty powder on the surface of the pot. This rubbed off easily and was so fluffy that it was difficult to paint on.   This problem for Mr Chapplow who, with advice from Stoke, before painting gave all the pots an additional low firing at 700 degrees Centigrade to 'harden' the glaze but not completely fuse it.   This enabled the pottery to be handled and painted easily.   It also allowed the pieces, not immediately needed, to be stacked in the warehouse without damage prior to painting .   A problem was solved but the additional time of loading, firing and unloading the pots increased the production costs.

Having been through this hardening-on firing, the pots went to the painting room.   Usually the Traditional range was painted in three stages.   The expert painters, Jessie Bambury, Florrie Richards and later Doreen Moat and Katie Richards would 'draw out' the outline of the pattern arranging the flowers and fitting them to the shape of the pot.   The outlined pattern would then be passed to a 'filler in' who would select the colours of her choice in the case of the Jacobean Pattern or follow the standard colours of Persian and the Border patterns.   Finally the pot would be banded, if necessary, and have the dots applied.   It was impressive to see how quickly and skilfully the experts did this.

The Border patterns, numbers 3 to 12 were started by the bands being applied on a wheel. An interesting simple but clever device was used.   The edge of the banding wheel was marked with a variety of coloured lines.   Each colour related to a number of divisions of a circle.   According to the pot being painted, there could be anything from four repeats on an egg cup to twelve repeats around a plate.   The coloured lines ensured the correct number of pencil marks could be put round the pot to guide the person 'drawing out' the design to fit it on to the pot.

The painted pots with raw colour on them were very easily smudged before firing and, believe me, however many notices asking visitors "Do NOT touch, these pots will smudge" there were always some people who wanted to see if they really did!

The pottery staff had to devise clever ways of picking things up to avoid smudging. Instead of holding the painted outside of a vase they put their fingers inside carefully without touching the dots on the top. The pots were then loaded on to the kiln truck and fired to the gloss temperature. Later, the next afternoon, the moment of truth, and hopefully joy, as the kiln was opened and all the previously dusty looking colours showed their fully glory.

As time progressed from the 1960's the Painting room was used, apart from the Traditional designs, for many techniques and processes of decorating for our many different ranges.

For many years a speciality of the Pottery was the decorating of Commemorative plates with personalised gold and silver lettering. We designed a set of six 'centres' and had special gold and silver transfers made. Around these we hand lettered whatever the person wanted for their special individual plate using liquid real gold or platinum for silver. This required a high degree of calligraphic skill. The main designers were Julian Roebuck, Allison Wilmington, Caroline Wright and Bridget Hillyard. It was essential to 'vent' the kiln (keep the chimney open) until reached 350 degrees C. when firing all transfers and any gold painting. This was to release the fumes from the cover coat and gold solvent medium otherwise the decorations did not fire to a true brightness. The fumes made a really horrid smell!

In 1980 an Offset Pad Printing machine, the latest high technology in ceramic decoration, was purchased. The design detail was 120 mesh to the inch, a very fine photographic quality. Etchings of designs were reproduced onto photopolymer plates. The process relied on very critical surface adhesion of the ceramic colours. They had to be prepared in a special medium and worked only when heated. The etching was mounted on a heated plate. Colour was applied, a scraper removed the excess. The pad was lowered to the etching and the colour picked up by the pad, lifting the design. The pad moved and was then lowered on to the pottery piece. The image left the pad and was transferred to the pot. As you can imagine it required skill and technology to obtain a perfect image. If the temperatures were not correct the image could stay in the etching, or stay on the pad and not appear on the pot! For years the major Stoke potteries had been trying to print with a type of Gelatine pad which had a very short working life and frequently split. It was the advent of Silicone rubber for the pad that made the process viable and possible. The pads cost more than £100 each but had a life of several thousand

prints instead of one hundred plus with gelatine.   The machine gave us a new market for souvenirs and commemorative items which became a substantial part of our turnover.

Our expert machine operator was Pam Lane who printed many thousands of pieces.   They included all of the Charles and Diana Wedding design and the commemoratives for the birth of the Princes, souvenirs of London (Tower Bridge, Westminster Abbey, Tower of London etc.), countless towns and cities, Honiton of course, and commemoratives for Rotary Clubs, sporting clubs, County Shows, National Trust properties, towns twinning and even to celebrate a person's hundredth birthday.

Ceramic transfers were printed or 'screen printed' with special ceramic colours on to gummed paper and had a special 'cover coat' applied.   This bonded to the colours to enable them to lift off the paper, when immersed in water, and to be applied to the pot.   In general this was the easiest way to apply decorations to pottery.   If the item had a plain flat surface the transfer was applied and the surface stroked with a squeegee to remove the water.   If the shape was curved in various ways, as on a vase, then the pot and the transfer had to be warmed to make the 'cover coat' flexible enough to be coaxed round the curves.   It required skill to avoid tucks and tears and to ensure the transfer was firmly on the surface without any air bubbles underneath.   There were many 'open stock' transfers available which we used for some ranges such as 'Harvest' but in general we commissioned our own exclusive designs and had them specially printed.   After application, the pots were ready for their firing. Pad printing and the gold lettered commemorative plates were also fired at about 760 degrees Centigrade. This is because these colours and metals would not withstand higher temperatures.

After the final firing and a final check, if passed, they would head for the warehouse and packing or if a 'second' to our shop for sale to visitors.

In the 1960s Ray Boyland and Arthur Long shared the packing job in unpleasant working conditions but it was not long before we rearranged things for them to be in the main building. The pottery was packed in large cartons in straw, which was purchased from local farmers.   We tried to find good, clean, long straw because short, brittle, dusty straw with brambles and thorns, was very unkind to the hands and not popular with packers or customers.   We carefully laid out the orders and double checked them before and during packing.   There were many occasions when customers reported tea pot lids or small items missing.   We knew they had been packed but the customer, knee deep in straw in the middle of their shop, could not find the needle in the haystack!   As we all know the customer is always right!

It was also not long before we changed to wood wool as a packing material and this was eventually superseded by dimple paper and bubble wrap. Packing pottery was always been a problem so in the 1980s the Pottery industry set up a system of 'trays'. These were of stout cardboard and could be filled with pots wrapped only in paper. There was a special nation wide delivery service door to door which supposedly eliminated the breakage and non-delivery problems.

When the tour was completed the visitors were directed towards the showroom. Before we purchased the houses on the High Street, it was in the corrugated building which was also the works office and the garage for No. 30. During the summer months there were quite a number of visitors and sales but, during the winter, it was rather sparse. I recall that in our trading rush in Christmas week of 1961 the Showroom total takings were £5. When the shop was on the High Street sales were appreciably better.

In 1963, No 30 High Street came on the market and we were pleased to buy it. It was the house previously lived in by Charles Collard. As we converted it into the pottery shop, we revealed the old stone front wall and brick fireplaces   At this time the West Country holiday trade was flourishing .

During the summer months the shop was so busy that we really needed more space. No 32 became available which we purchased. It was helpful to have the additional space but the shop was in two part on either side of the entrance. It was sad to see potential customers going away having only been in one part!

As production increased with the new machinery so did the 'seconds' and the need for the shop became even greater. There were tremendous bargains because we had to clear the stock. We spent a great deal of time and thought making the shop attractive and interesting. In 1981, we eventually managed to purchase No 34 High street which had a 'right of way' through the pottery entrance to the back of the property. This had prevented us closing the entrance gap and joining our two shops together. It was a planning condition that we had to improve the side entrance to the pottery site between No. 18 and 20 High Street, if we closed the gap between the shops. So in 1981, one hundred years after it was noted that James Webber started a pottery on the site, that we enlarged the shop. To celebrate this we painted, in Traditional Honiton Design, a large tile panel for the front wall. Everyone employed at the pottery at the time painted a piece of it. The main work was by Allison Wilmington. A copy of the design and the list of all the staff was presented to the Honiton Museum as a record and for safe keeping.

The Honiton Pottery name and the production equipment was sold to Dartmouth Pottery in 1992. They removed all the master moulds and equipment to their factory where they continued production.   The shop was reduced in size and No 32 and No 34 were sold to the Devon County Council and No 30 , The Honiton Pottery Shop was leased to Mr.& Mrs Wallis.

The Honiton Pottery name and the production equipment was sold to Dartmouth Pottery in 1992. They removed all the master moulds and equipment to their factory where they continued production.   The shop was reduced in size and No 32 and No 34 were sold to the Devon County Council and No 30 , The Honiton Pottery Shop was leased to Mr.& Mrs Wallis.

The Pottery Ranges,
And notes on the Designers and some Customers.

The majority of people using this book will be mainly interested in identifying the pottery items made at Honiton to establish the age and the other details associated with their 'find'. Therefore the following is a list of the primary products produced with only a few anecdotes and comments that seem appropriate to me. They are not listed in order of importance to the Pottery nor are they in any special order date because many ranges overlapped other ranges in time of production. We were proud to produce all of them.

The sales catalogues of Charles Collard are interesting to compare with those of a later date by the Hulls and the Chapplows. Prior to 1947 there were no slip cast items because this process was introduced to Honiton by Norman Hull. The clay was changed and throwing was phased out.

During the period, 1961-1992, there were no "thrown" items with the "Traditional" decoration style nor was any quantity of red, terra cotta clay used. Therefore all Traditional thrown pieces, whatever the clay, and all brown or brownish clay pieces are prior to 1961.

The majority of the later pieces were slip cast which is easy to identify as different from thrown pieces. If you look inside you will see that in cast pieces the inside profile exactly follows the outside shape which is especially noticeable inside at the foot. A thrown pot shape flows round and does not have a hollow in the foot ring. If the handle has been cast in one with the pot there is always a telltale casting mark on the inside which helps identify this production method. Therefore, when dating a piece, you can be sure that Traditional Designs on cast pots were made after 1947.

Round plates and dishes were made on the 'Jolly', until 1968, (details of the production method are elsewhere in the book) and then the Ram Press was introduced, the 'jolly' discarded, and all the shapes changed. This may again help to identify the age of the piece.

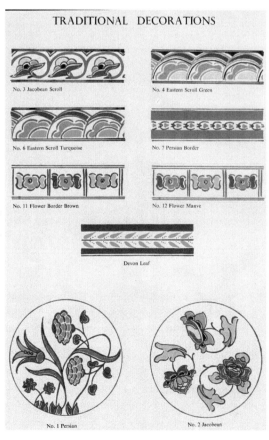

48

HONITON POTTERY LTD.
TRADITIONAL DECORATIONS

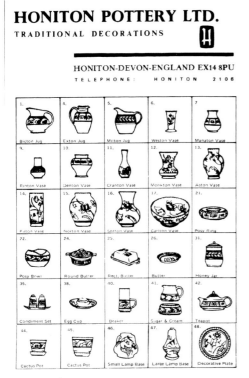

HONITON-DEVON-ENGLAND EX14 8PU
TELEPHONE: HONITON 2106

In most cases it is possible to identify the painter by the numbers and letters underneath. The first initial is the person 'drawing out' or outlining, the second is the person 'filling in' and the number (on border patterns) is the design number. A list of painters is elsewhere.

The sheets illustrated show Traditional decorations and the variety of products available from the 1960s. Honiton Pottery was one of the few Potteries in the country which considered design a very important part of the Pottery. It is perhaps for this reason that it outlived almost all the small, semi commercial Potteries in the West Country. There are notes about some of the people who contributed to the many and various models, shapes and designs created and used by and at Honiton Pottery during the period from 1961 to 1992.

Early in the 1960's it became evident that the sales of the Traditional Honiton were inadequate to support the pottery production.

Therefore we adopted a general design policy which held good until the Pottery production was sold in 1992. It was unrealistic to compete with the factories in Stoke making mass production items so we tried to produce hand crafted and hand painted pottery at affordable prices efficiently. Most of the Studio potters had limited facilities and could not satisfy the needs of the West Country gift shop tourist trade of the time.

I studied Studio pottery at the Bournemouth Municipal College of Art obtaining a National Diploma in Design and an A.T.D. I taught pottery and art before coming to Honiton. As Managing Director I was in overall control of the design policy, selecting designers and their designs for production. I added the Devon Leaf design to the Traditional range, designed the Jennifer Range and most of the Craftsman range. Latterly I designed several other products including the Rowena Children's range and the Petunia which I also hand painted.

Jennifer Range was our first attempt to introduce completely new designs. Useful holiday gifts were in demand. We designed this new 'stylish' shape for slip casting. The side was scratched with a piece of hacksaw blade, in true studio pottery style, and a raw oxide colour was brushed boldly on so that it showed as a darker colour in the grooves. This created our intended studio pottery effect.

It was a small range of items and we sold thousands; salts and peppers in two sizes, mustard pots, cruet bases, honey pot, two sizes of dish, coffee mugs and table lamps.

Ultimately table lamps in the Jennifer range generated huge orders. Cookstone Royle one of the countries largest table lamp shade manufacturing companies at that time ordered a specially designed range with the Jennifer decoration.   It was sold under their name in many department stores.

Michael Emmett B.A. joined as a studio potter and designer.   His excellent hand throwing skill was used making large pieces, pedestal planters and lamp bases, particularly with a splattered glaze.   The **Woodbury range** he designed was originally hand-thrown to obtain an authentic form.   This was then cast and produced by the Pottery. This range was converting wheel thrown and 'cut' shapes into cast items to create the attractive studio pottery effect.   For example the mug was thrown and the handle applied.   This was allowed to dry to leather hard then filled with plaster of Paris.   With care, a mould was then made of the clay shape and then that mould was filled with plaster to make a plaster 'master'.   Then the usual mould making process of 'blocking' and 'casing' was done to enable production moulds to be made.   The range included two sizes of mug, sugar bowls, cream jugs, coffee pots, wine goblets and wine carafes.   A long process but it created the right effect.   Saucers were made on the Ram press.   Working with glaze chemists in Stoke, we devised the attractive speckled sandy matt glaze.   The pot was sprayed with this then the top of the piece was over-sprayed with a matt brown glaze.   The insides of the mugs were glazed with a white gloss glaze to avoid a grating noise when stirring coffee and to make it easy to clean. For a few customers we glazed the range in a shining rich Rockingham brown glaze.

Michael Caddy Cookware   We decided to produce cookware in order to increase our sales in a different direction and invited Michael Caddy to design for us. He created some very strange rather impractical shaped casseroles but alas his designs would not sell. We therefore designed our own shapes, so was born our "Craftsman Range".

For cookware we had to develop the right firing techniques and skills to make the suitable quality ceramic.

Craftsman Range of oven-to-tableware.   This was undoubtedly the most important range produced at Honiton from 1966.   It started with a set of casseroles; 5 pint, 3 pint and 2 pint.   Then were added the inevitable cruets and a lidded onion soup bowl.   The first item to be made on the Ram Press was an oval plate.   This really made the range a winner because at the time there were not any good reasonably priced oval plates on the market.   We developed the basic range quickly. The plate shape, with a 'stand up' edge, was quite different from others on sale; luckily for us it was very popular.

Although the range is important in the history of the pottery it is probably not of great interest to collectors because it was not a decorative item.   It was mainly produced in plain colours. Initially it was produced in a mottled blue with brown flecks, very much a 'studio' look, however it was too inconsistent for commercial place settings of tableware. It was made in Matt Brown and Devon Red, which were the most popular colours. Other versions were a glossy amber, glossy peat green and matt blue.

When the Pizzaland group started the restaurant chain our matt brown was chosen. We supplied them for about two years but then the demand for all the new restaurants opening became too much for us. We supplied many restaurants in various parts of the country with our Craftsman. Apart from gift shops and china shops several department stores sold it such as Dingles, Boots and even Harrods.

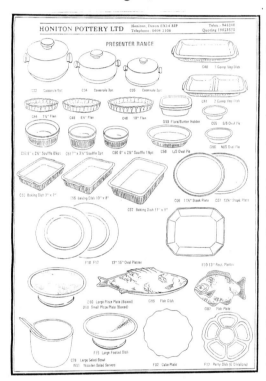

The "Craftsman" developed into a comprehensive range of tableware and cookware items as the various illustrations show.

The basic shapes were used for all our other products. Traditional painted plates, souvenirs, commemoratives, Aldermaston, Jane Willingale and all the others.

Aldermaston hand painted cookware is illustrated earlier. I met Alan Caiger-Smith, the master potter of Aldermaston Pottery in Berkshire; early in the 1970s and after a little discussion, we agreed to work together on a tableware project. His wonderful brushwork designs were and are very popular but his production was limited because he not only painted the pottery but he made it all himself. He had an order for a restaurant and was unable to fulfil it. We used our Craftsman shapes and developed a new cup shape similar to his. He came to Honiton and we developed similar colours to his and he showed the painters his techniques. Florrie Richards

was instantly capable of painting the designs so the project went ahead. This was another example of creating good studio pottery commercially. The range of Aldermaston designs included not only tableware on a white glaze but also on our stoneware glaze The design worked well on table lamps. We used the Jennifer shapes because they had the ideal plain flat sides to decorate. These lamps must be interesting to collectors.

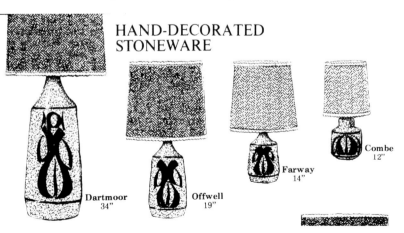

HAND-DECORATED
STONEWARE

Dartmoor
34"

Offwell
19"

Farway
14"

Combe
12"

51

Hembury was small range on a pinkish glaze with a delicate soft pink flower which was based on a pencil drawing designed by **Nora Cowell**. It was an ideal design for pad printing as seen here.

We used our skills with hand painting to decorate many of our Craftsman and cookware shapes. Most noteworthy were the very decorative large platters with fish and turkey designs. In the Cookware range we also had Chicken lids in a variety of coloured effects and rather unusual chicken jugs.

David, Marquis of Queensbury (Professor of Design, R.C.A.) It was hoped that he, with his design partner Martin Hunt, would create a new tableware range. We met him at Trade Shows because he had designed the very successful range of Suffolk Kitchen for Watson's Pottery. He designed some very elegant cups and saucers but that was as far as it went. Perhaps it was due to his commitments with major Stoke manufacturers and other large potteries that he did not have his heart in designing for Honiton.

Calman Cookery. Mel Calman, the late cartoonist of the Times Newspaper, had written a humorous cookery book with his charming drawings on various cooking topics. I contacted him at The Cartoon Gallery in London and we agreed that some of his designs would decorate some of our cookware shapes. The basic Craftsman shapes were used and the design applied by ceramic transfers which we had specially made. There were six cartoon designs in the set which we applied to a variety of pieces. I still enjoy the gentle humour. The range was first made in 1983 and sold well for several years but withdrawn from selling to the trade in 1989; it was then sold only in the pottery shop at Honiton.

Goff Cartoons. To augment the Calman range and to offer new cartoon products to customers we contacted Geoff Motley. We produced a few of the Goff's cartoons on cookware but they were not as well received and only a few were produced. I think by this time the vogue for ceramic cookware had passed the peak. The flan dishes with recipes and decorations had over-filled the shops.

Hi Tech. We still wanted to keep the tableware going by adding new finishes. Therefore we tried a high gloss black version with a red or yellow rim giving a very dramatic effect. There was always a last minute rush to show new items so we hurriedly prepared samples with the red edge for the Harrogate Gift Fair. It looked smart and we took orders. Our son, Simon, was impressed by it. As he was about to go to university he decided to have our Hi Tech range to use in his room. He took the show samples and some extra pieces. Imagine his alarm when the red edge washed off some of the items. They only had poster paint edges because there was not time to apply ceramic colours and fire them before the show. It was on general sale during the mid 1980s.

Transfer decorated and other versions of the Craftsman Range were in demand as plain matt colours became less fashionable. We therefore offered several transfer decorated ranges including Hydrangea and Harvest Both ranges used open stock transfers and were useful as extra sales for the shapes. Hydrangea was on a brilliant white gloss glaze and Harvest on the special glaze developed for our souvenir and countryside products.

Christmas Ranges. Because we had a Ram Press and the Stoke potters had not bought one we were better able to make oval, fluted and non-round shaped dishes. Therefore we made a vast quantity of Christmas Pottery for Cuthbertsons in the United States which was produced with their back stamp and called Original Christmas. The orders would be for 2,000 to 5,000 of each item and would be shipped throughout the year. The shapes included various sizes of Oval platters, rectangular platters, fluted edge cake plates, Christmas tree shapes and a variety of tree decorations. The Cuthbertson range was exclusive to them so we could not sell any Seconds. They had to be sent to them with the regular stock, at half the price!

However a Christmas range of our own seemed a good idea. Cuthbertsons was so successful that we produced our range for U.K. Sales. Our range did not compete with Cuthbertsons because his customers were all in the US. Ours was a success too although, perhaps, not highly collectable but look for our back stamp! We created ours using holly and Christmas tree transfer designs. It was very popular possibly because it was about half the price of the Spode range!

Countryside Range. It was a limited giftware selection, on a matt nutmeg coloured glaze of various birds and selection of flowers. They were very attractive transfers. We produced various dishes, coasters, mugs and teapot stands.

Julie's Range of fun Egg cups. **Julie Galuszka** joined us straight from university and designed cars and planes as egg cups. Not only was the design outstanding but she modelled them brilliantly. They were produced on the Ram press which enabled us to make hundreds quite quickly.

We chose bright colours, had little transfers made for the aeroplane wings and painted the cars headlights with platinum/silver. For the Spring Giftware Show at the National Trade Centre, Birmingham Julie built a fun roadway for the cars with hills covered with bright felts and she stuck the planes on a blue felt sky with white cloud shapes.

They were outstandingly successful. If I remember correctly we took about £8,000 worth of orders at that show. She eventually added to the range boats. tortoises, and for little children, Teddy Bears, Chickens, and Rabbits. You may find Table lamps with small planes or cars and a fun vapour trail. Having developed the range it was known as 'Functional Fun'.

Julie was possibly the most talented designer we employed. She also modelled our range of animal money boxes of which the pony was an outstanding success. However we were surprised at one trade show to get a large order for the Hippo. It came from the Henley Rowing Club who had a hippo as their emblem in pink!

Her stylised designs of Dumpdon, the hill overlooking the town, were the basis of some souvenir and tableware designs. She hand carved a delicately embossed plant form creating our Hedgerow range. This was another example of her modelling skills. Items included powder bowls, bathroom accessories, vases and table lamps which were very popular. . The relief modelling was enhanced and made to show to its full charm by the subtle translucent pampas colour glaze or the bolder Rockingham glaze. Our Owl lamps were yet another product designed and modelled by Julie.

We experimented with pressing terra cotta clay for cookware ranges. We produced a range of Pizza dishes with a relief form of the Traditional pattern embossed on the base. It proved difficult to keep the red clay from contaminating our white clay so, although the product was a success, it was too problematic to continue.

Loudware. Jane Willingale a designer and part–time ceramics lecturer, was unable, in her small studio, to fulfil her orders because her designs were so popular. At first we produced blank shapes for her and when she saw our painting skills, she asked us to produce and market the ranges of tulip and daffodil designs in her unique style. They were produced for several years by our expert painters We tried other of her designs of

various animals, dogs pigs etc. but they were not so successful. Jane decided they she wanted to keep her hand painting exclusive to herself so withdrew our agreement to paint her designs.

Meanwhile, the Next Store Group had commissioned Jane to design a small hand painted range for their stores. She was unable to consider this volume of work in her studio so, as she was working with us at this time, we agreed to make and decorate them to her design. The range consisted of four 'Face Plates', and a yellow Jug and vase with a black outline face. It was a limited production run and the plates proved especially popular.

Hinchcliffe and Barber. We made blanks for them to decorate in their studio and we produced a limited range of their designs for them. As with any expensive hand painted designs the volumes were not very great.

Devonmoor Blue Mugs. We only started producing these after we purchased the mug machine from Devonmoor Pottery. It was not our intention to make their mugs but the demand

from their customers was so great that we agreed. These mugs were dipped in blue slip and the names scratched through to show the white clay base. We used their moulds and matched their blue slip. Our clay was more highly fired because it was used for tableware and cookware. The mugs turned out slightly smaller and stronger. Devonmoor customers had always bought a few blank mugs to etch in their shop if they had a missing name. Our mugs were so strong they could not scratch them! This was not popular. As well as people's names we made a number of fun names and hundreds of town

names. This part of the general gift business was being overtaken by cheap multicoloured mugs. Hand scratching the names on to the unfired mugs required an attractive hand writing style and accuracy of spelling.

Floral 80's. This was a small range of very positive deeply modelled plant pots and dishes. They were designed mainly by Michael Emmett who created them. They were slip cast and initially plain white. Later we produced these hand painted Speciality pieces.

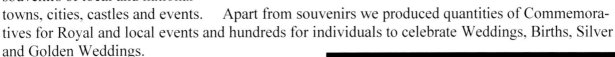

Souvenirs and Commemoratives. Over a period of more than twenty five years we made thousands of souvenirs of local and national towns, cities, castles and events. Apart from souvenirs we produced quantities of Commemoratives for Royal and local events and hundreds for individuals to celebrate Weddings, Births, Silver and Golden Weddings.

Our first serious entry into the market was in 1970 with our range of 'Honipots'. **David Harris**, an illustrator and lecturer in commercial design at Exeter College of Art created the very attractive designs. We had ceramic transfers produced in a deep blue colour. Our sales agents sold them to many tourist places. David Harris also designed the Mayflower 1970 plate from which we created a silk screen image. This was an exciting technique requiring skill and confidence. Flimsy tissue paper was laid on a table. Black ceramic ink, with a vile smell, was heated, applied to the silk screen and pressed through on to the paper. While the ink was warm this delicate paper was reversed and lowered on to the unfired

glazed plate. This transferred the image. Where it touched, right or wrong, the design stayed. Hand rubbing pressed the rest of the design on the surface. The colours were then hand painted and the pottery re-fired. This technique was used for many other projects including in 1970 we also produced souvenirs to commemorate the death of Thomas Becket in Canterbury.

NUTMEG (SATIN) GLAZE   ALMOND (GLOSS) GLAZE

Some special transfer designs were produced for The City of Exeter, Honiton Borough Council, East Devon District as well as for International Folk Festivals but they are too many to identify them all here.

Julian Roebuck   After retiring as an Art Director for the J. Walter Thompson Group he came to live in Honiton.   He designed the hand painted fish and bird range of dishes, which we have illustrated earlier, using the Mayflower Plate technique, many thousands of these dishes and plates were produced and sold.   His charming drawings of children did not sell in large quantities.   They are quite rare! He was a fine graphic designer who created many of our main souvenir and commemorative designs of the 1970s and 80s.   These included the Wedding of Charles and Diana and birth plate designs for their children, the Wedding of Andrew & Sarah, Exeter's 900 year plates, the visit of the Pope and many more.

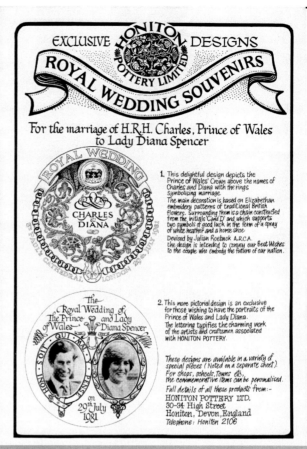

As mentioned in the works tour we purchased the Offset Pad Printer because of the growing demand for 'Specials'.   This was a state of the art machine which could print designs up to nine inches diameter.   It was just in time for the Royal Wedding the following year.

Table Lamps and shades.   Apart from the lamps made in the Jennifer range for Crookson Royale there were numerous contracts with companies such Phillipinalia, Bushell and Saward, Jeff Uren and store groups such as Boots. We needed to have shades to match and/or coordinate so we set up our own lampshade making department and produced thousands of shades.   This was arranged under the guidance and expertise of Jennie Redvers as mentioned

before.

Jackie Scott's Birds. This young designer, who studied ceramics at Camberwell College of Art, created the fresh design of stylised Birds on a stylised treetop nest. It is a very cheerful design in just the one colourway.   It was produced on a limited number of shapes, coffee and beer mugs, large and small plates and a large cereal bowl.   She also designed our **Tropical**

range. This was basically an outline screen printed tropical jungle scene with exotic plants, birds and animals, which was then hand painted in bright colours. We took pieces of the design to decorate items so each was individually different as illustrated in the appendix.

Roses by Joanna Barringer.   Her bold hand painted designs of Roses were started in the last few years of pottery production at Honiton. It had very little national coverage but was the mainstay of the newer hand painting designs the shop sold into the 90's. It is an excellent all over design, mainly painted by Caroline Walker, who was able to obtain and maintain very lively brushstrokes.   It was produced in several slightly different colour versions. It should be greatly enjoyed by collectors.

Caroline Walker and Martin Lloyd were both designers who worked for us in the painting area and developed the production designs of many souvenirs and adding to our various ranges.

I designed a small range of children's items, called **Rowena**, with a main motif of Sheep, Owls or Pigs which were pad printed in several colours. They then had hand painted details and bold brush colour areas added.

I also designed our **Up-lighter Children's Bedside lights** with clown faces, planes, trains and cottages with holes lighting the windows and eyes.   These lamps proved an interesting attractive alternative to other s on the market and added to the wide range of general table lamps which we produced.

Contract Production.

Flower Arrangement pieces. The first range we produced was for Elaine Goddard.   This was a selection of classic shaped vases.   They were delicate and subtle unlike many so the rather clumsy ones made by some potters.   The pedestal vases were particularly popular.

Flower Beauty   As we were involved with flowers arrangers we were approached by a party plan company, with a head office in the U.S., selling plastic pinholders. They required, for their UK party plan sales group, a selection of unusual and exclusive shapes for their Ikebana displays and sales.   The company demonstrated flower arrangements in peoples homes and sold their pin holders and our pots. There was nothing like it at the time. We designed most of them to be made on the Ram Press and so could produce them in volume and at a reasonable price.   This lasted several years and sold many thousands of pots.   Some of these are pictured earlier on page 15.

Ceramics and Crystal.   This was an importer and wholesaler with a large team of salesmen for whom we made a wide range of hand painted flower vases.   There were special shapes, mainly footed vases and plant pots painted with a bold brushwork leaf design under coloured transparent high gloss glazes or matt glazes with similar on-glaze painting.

Advertising ashtrays, jugs, mugs etc.
        Over the years we made many thousands of such items. These are just a few companies and the products; for **Rothman** we made square black ashtrays, for **Watney** we made round ones, for **Benson and Hedges** we made cube shaped black ice-check jugs, for **Taunton Cider** we made a special range of reproduction cider mugs for their Museum sales.   Very few products had our back stamp on them so, even if found, can not be easily identified.

For Van Den Bergs, the makers of **Flora**, we produced many hundreds of two sizes of container for their plastic tubs.

Heatherly Fine China.
This firm made, or at least sold, bathroom fittings and bathroom accessories, jars, soap dishes etc. which we made for them under contract in a variety of soft colours with various delicate ceramic transfers.

Euchre Trophies.
These were specially commissioned by Ginger Taylor of the British Euchre Association and sponsored by Taunton CIder.   We produced a hand holding a group of playing cards 'the ideal euchre hand' which we made as lids for mugs and tankards,.   We wrote 'Winner', 'Runner up' and other things for them.   They were very popular and we made them dozens at a time for about ten years.

Mr Paul Redvers, right, and Ray Boyland, of Honiton Pattery, show "Ginger" Taylor and his wife, Diane, the trophies for the British Euchre Association Championship which were commissioned from the pottery.

POTTERY PROVIDES TROPHIES

Puzzles and Paradoxes. We produced a limited range for James Dalgetty of special ceramics. They included Puzzle Jugs in royal blue with special gold transfers, and 'Rabbiducks' which looked like a rabbit until turned on its side then it became a duck!

Wessex Pottery. This was a Party Plan scheme run by Len Younger from Bournemouth. The range was decorated with flowing glazes. There were base colours of either amber or Rockingham brown with a reactive white glaze over the top. We used mainly our own shapes such as Woodbury goblets and our Craftsman range but had some special mugs of his own design. At the height of his business he was collecting a van load from us every week.

Carla Pottery.
This was a Party Plan scheme run by Paul Turner from his Bristol warehouse. We used our basic shapes and decorated them with a special cream glaze which was transfer decorated with a delicate lily design. Some special shapes were also made. He ran a very efficient business and sold large quantities of our pottery. It ran for most of the 1980s. He made a video of our production to show to his sales team which, I believe, is the best photographic record of our production.

Crescendo Memento
The graphic artist, Robert Jennings, provided beautiful delicate pencil drawings of the Best of Breed dogs and special Breeds of Horses. Because we had the very efficient and precise pad printing facility we

were able to reproduce the sensitive drawings with great accuracy. We made a comprehensive range for him on our nutmeg matt glaze.

Elliott Toby Jugs. There were four different designs used by the building company as a Christmas gift to promote their business to people in local government and politics. There were several other designs planned but alas the company went bust! They were very collectable and fun mugs designed by Alan Bailey and modelled by Barry Ward. There were about 500 made of each character.

Maryse Boxer. The range which takes her name is truly an outstanding piece of design collaboration between a designer and a pottery with design flair. She advertised to find a pottery to produce her ideas and Honiton was the only British Pottery to respond to the venture. This dramatic range was based on Japanese simplicity, with square, lotus and round plates initially in black or white. It was acclaimed in the high fashion stores of the 1980's. The range eventually had not only those shapes in various sizes but also huge serving platters, large and small heart shapes, salad bowls and cups and saucers. It was glazed and some were hand painted in various colours.

King Rollo Film Company.
It was based in Honiton. Their delightful merry cartoon characters were ideal for a children's range. We had transfers made and we decorated bowls mugs and dishes. Although attractive and we sold quite a lot we were not able to get the range into any of the really big distributors.

Other customers
We produced for many other companies; Candlesticks for **Prices Candles**, pots for **Coleman's Mustard**, Hot top Butter Softeners for **John Hunt**, Mugs for **Perry's Cider** and for **Sheepy's Cider**.

Imperial War Museum we made oval pie dishes with the Second War recipe for Walton Pie, forThe Cabinet Rooms we made pint mugs with a picture of Churchill.
We put logos on items for the Basil Hotel London, Coffee Pot restaurants, Chaucer's Restaurant, Exeter. We sold souvenirs to Selfridges, Morwellham Quay, The National Trust, Bath Postal Museum, Buckfast Abbey, The Oxford Collection and Crested Mugs for a great many RAF Squadrons.
We made special designs for hundreds of towns, shops and restaurants, some illustrations are in the appendix.

Our Export customers which have not been mentioned earlier included:- Barneys of New York, Apex Inc. Japan, Aventi in Helsinki, Macys New York, Aventura in New York, LEC in Japan, Gallerie La

Fayette in Paris, O K in Malta, Barneys in Japan, and Sazaby in Japan. Some more details of these are also in the appendix.

Further colour sheets and details of the products which would have overpowered the text are also part of the appendix.

After the closure of the factory in 1992 we continued to produce a limited amount of hand painting in the shop. We had retained this aspect of the business. I designed and painted, "Petunia". It was completely freehand pained and only by me. The blank glazed pieces were bought-in , some earthenware and some fine bone china.

We also continued with our commemorative plates, house name plates, and other personalised items trading as "Signature of Honiton"/

A tribute must be paid to our very tolerant , efficient and co-operative staff; the modellers, mould makers, casters, fettlers whose jobs were frequently modified as products and techniques changed. Also the sprayers and kiln loading team who accepted any pots which needed their attention. Also the highly skilled painters who changed styles from Traditional designs to many varied techniques and processes. They painted, transferred, stippled, sponged and pad printed designs. Not to be forgotten, the maintenance teams who kept the machines running and the kilns firing.

Honiton Pottery.

******

The Pottery Makers
And
The Office and Shop staff

*****

General List of the main Pottery workers at Honiton
From 1961 to 1992
with dates and jobs done.

I have put together a brief list of some of the many people who worked at the pottery over years. They are not listed in any order of importance and it is an incomplete record. It cannot include everyone and I know I have overlooked many who could well have been noted. If you, relatives or friends, do not appear it is not because of lacking importance. Our greatest asset was the staff of wonderful people who worked with and for us. Without them we would have had no Pottery business and it was through their skills and helpfulness that such varied interesting products were made. It was the Pottery team with their many expertises who were important. The Honiton Pottery Collectors Society has a detailed record of almost everyone and many photographs. In order to avoid unnecessary confrontation with the staff we always basically followed the Stoke potters holiday entitlement and their annual pay settlements. We worked on an hourly pay rates whereas Stoke, with their mass production techniques, mainly had piece rates. If I recall correctly, it was in the late 70s that one of the fettlers' husbands was a local official Transport and General Workers Union steward Unknown to me he was recruiting Union members in the town. The first I knew about it was when I had a call from ACAS, the Conciliation and Arbitration Service, asking if I wanted their help. I said I did not think so. They said that with the number of people we employed the workers were entitled to have Union recognition. They, our staff, intended to vote and select a Union. I should consider what would happen if the pottery staff were persuaded to join the T and G Workers Union. If we were to have a Union it seemed that the Ceramics Union was the most appropriate. I immediately contacted the Ceramics Union in Stoke. They were slightly surprised that a Managing Director would contact them and ask them to unionise a Pottery. They promptly sent a person to talk to the staff. For a few pence a week the staff paid their dues to the Ceramics Union and a possible militant confrontation was avoided.

I hope and believe the Pottery was a happy work environment which steadily improved from very basic conditions when we arrived in 1961 to being almost pleasant. As time progressed the work wear changed from rubber aprons over home clothes to clean white terylene outfits. Dust, although not a serious problem for us, with our wet clay processes, was well controlled by damp or wet washing of the premises to comply with the Factories Acts. We always did our best to ensure the health and welfare of the staff. Happily there were very few accidents at the Pottery, none were very serious, as could be seen in the Official Accident Register. Over the years a few people cut fingers on pots, stumbled and almost inevitably there were a few strained muscles. Not being unsympathetic but various reports such as "walked into a pile of plates, hurt leg" seems almost self inflicted and how do you explain the "flat trolley wheels hit ear ?!" and then "stung by wasp" is a lifestyle problem not a pottery hazard.

The people listed below are roughly grouped by length of service or job association.
David Hickmott He was one of Charles Collards highly skilled hand throwers. We only knew him as a good slip caster. He understood clay. He was a merry person and a good cartoon artist. Visitors to the pottery will no doubt recall his drawing by the stairs of a person tumbling down head first. I think he could not come to terms with the more mechanised processes and so left to work with Tom Sheriff at Axe Vale Pottery in Seaton.

Arthur Long. Started in 1946, when he left the Navy, loading the Bottle kiln and firing it with coal. During his time at the Pottery he did almost every job, with a great willingness and considerable skill. The exception, he was never seen hand painting. At various times he was packing, loading the electric kilns and maintaining them, glaze spraying, slip casting, Ram pressing, mould making and all the general production jobs.   It would be difficult to have found a more helpful employee.   Nothing was too much trouble. He retired in 1991.

Ray Boyland   He started in 1955, after he had left the Navy and had then been a baker in Honiton.   He took a temporary job at the Pottery and stayed and became a great leader of the pottery staff.   We sent him on a supervisor's course in Exeter and he eventually became our General Manager.   I think he liked to remember his time in the Navy when as a Petty Officer he was taught leadership and management of men.   He began packing, and, like Arthur, loading the electric kilns and maintaining them, replacing elements and fixing the many problems.   He was an excellent glaze sprayer.   He could slip cast pottery and he was good at Ram pressing and efficiently set the Ram Press   Because of this ability and efficiency in all the general production jobs the staff had great respect for him and worked well under his leadership.   He was never late and, except for holidays, had hardly a day off in all the years he worked at the Pottery.   He retired in 1989

Peter Costa   He suffered considerably as a Japanese prisoner during the war started at the pottery in 1954. He became our specialist in slip preparation, clay management and slip casting.   He ran the casting department very conscientiously and efficiently for many years. He adapted willingly and helpfully to all the changes in production techniques over the years. An example of his loyal attitude was when the Pottery closed for the Christmas period for two weeks, as was mentioned in the works tour.   Without being asked, Peter would come into the Pottery, in his own time, as often as he thought necessary, to switch on the blunger to ensure the clay was in a good condition ready to restart production after the holiday.   He retired in 1983.

Roy Boughton M I Ceram.   He was imported from Poole Pottery in 1983 as Works Manager to add some technical skills which we needed with our mechanisation with the mug making and other machines.   He was very useful for few years but ultimately moved on to a larger company in 1988.

John Pennell   Joined us in 1976 as assistant manager having trained at Stoke Technical College and worked in Stoke on Trent Potteries. He was very good technically and mechanically with knowledge of all the specialist pottery machinery. Without the skills he brought with him, having grown up in the Pottery industry, we would have floundered.   As a man brought up in Stoke he truly understood Pottery production. He left in 1984.

Cyril Loving   He was also one of the most loyal staff any company could wish to have. He started in 1960 and specialised in kiln loading.   The loader's aim was to fit as many pots as possible on the shelves, ensuring that they had at least an eighth of an inch between them so that they did not stick to each other.   Pottery had to be selected to be the same height so that they would fit between the shelves without wasting too much space.   All glazed pieces had to have the glaze wiped from their foot ring or they would stick to the kiln shelf.   I do not remember any pot which Cyril had set in the kiln sticking to the shelf.   He retired in 1980.

Wendy Long Daughter of Arthur Long joined us in 1978 she was a good general worker mainly replacing Cyril Loving when he retired as our kiln loader.   She eventually married John Pennell and left in 1986.

Derek Wakeley.   We needed more engineering skills and Derek was an expert. He knew about hydraulics and almost every aspect of machinery. Not only was engineering his job but it was also his hobby.   There were many machines to maintain, the Ram press, slip pumps, pad printers, sponging machines, auto sprayers, handle spongers, etc...   He also helped to develop such essen-

tial machines as the belt spongers, the handle spongers and the engravers.   He was always helpful and invaluable, keeping the equipment going. He joined in 1984 and was with us until 1991.
Barry Ansell   A good mould maker was essential so he was employed from the early 1960s. He had trained and worked as a mould maker in Stoke on Trent.   His wife, also a skilled pottery worker, worked with us as a fettler.   They served us well for some years.   He made master and production moulds but they decided they missed their family and friends in Stoke and so returned home.

We decided we had, by now, enough local knowledge to do our own mould making so we employed **a** local person.

Mike Hendrick   He was a studio potter by training who took over the mould making and modelled most of the initial Craftsman shapes which we made.   A very capable person who decided, after a while not unreasonably, that he actually wanted to be a studio potter.   He left and set up a Studio Pottery in Charmouth,

Barry Ward   Joined to replace Mike and became a highly skilled and a very accurate mould maker.   He made all of theRam moulds, master models and working moulds.   He made slip casting masters and the slip casting moulds.   He worked in plaster, epoxy resin and silicone rubbers. Not only did he make moulds but also modelled the entire Maryse Boxer range and most of our plant pots and vases produced in later years.   He modelled our complete range of Post boxes and Flower beauty items.   He started at the pottery in about 1968 and stayed until the pottery closed in 1994.   It is difficult to overestimate his value to the pottery.

Charlie Pye A helpful local who was a Caster.   When Alf Johnson left he took over the Jolly making. An important process making all the 'flat' items before we had the Ram Press. He was with us from about 1965 to 1970 he left because he wanted to work in the open air and he became a milkman.   His wife Peggy worked for us as a fettler for many years.

Ben Kennett   As we employed more than twenty people we were required to employ a registered disabled person. We had Ben from 1974 to 1992.   He was completely deaf and had very little reading ability. He could just recognise his name, BEN, on his overalls! What could we do with him? We initially set him with the Casters and Mould making.   He was like jack-in-a-box.   He would not sit still or stay in one place.   He tried to be helpful everywhere so eventually we decided to let him do whatever job he wanted.   He proved to be one of the hardest most efficient workers anyone could wish to employ.   He ran everywhere, into the Pottery in the morning and ran out in the evening.   He helped everyone and intelligently loaded kilns and had a wonderful nature.   Because of his deafness, in order to attract attention to what he wanted or what he was doing he would let out a very loud, bloodcurdling squeal.   Many times visitors to the Pottery were alarmed and horrified by the noise.   They were relived and laughed when they heard the explanation.

Martin Lloyd   Joined in 1986 from Leicester Poly with a B.A in 3D design. He worked with the painters and worked on new designs and eventually became our decorating manager. He left in 1991.

Some of our designer/painters such as Julie Cummins are already noted in the section about our product ranges so are not noted here.

Caroline Walker   Ceramic designer from Birmingham Poly joined in 1981. She made a great contribution to the quality of painting. She drew many of the illustrations on our souvenirs which she translated from postcards. She was an expert at lettering on our personalised commemorative and house name plates.

Jessie Bambury She worked for Charles Collard initially. Of the hand painters she was possibly the most noted. She painted until her untimely death from cancer in the 1970s. She was somewhat eccentric, extrovert as is necessary to be a local dramatic actress. She also kept goats and often arrived for work in her wellies! I understand that she joined the pottery from school as a hand painter and became certainly one of the most skilful of our hand painters. Her large dishes with Persian and Jacobean designs were outstanding. Look for the initials on Traditional design pieces. JB

Florrie Richards A contemporary of Jessie also joined the pottery from school as a hand painter. Less flamboyant than Jessie but comparably skilful with her delicacy in 'drawing out' Traditional patterns. She had a natural gift for balancing the floral designs to fill a plate or go round a vase. She signed her pots F.R. When we introduced the Aldermaston Range designed by Alan Caiger Smith, Florrie was an instant expert at his brushwork designs.

Allison Wilmington. Joined in 1977 and from 1990 became part time. She was an excellent painter but her special skill was as a calligrapher. She was our specialist on commemorative plates for many years.

Katie Richards and Doreen Moat were both good hand painters with special drawing-out skills. They were the main stays of the painting room for many years. There must be many hundreds of pots with their initials on the base.

Mary Ebdon Another painter with particular expertise in painting bands on pottery and specialised painting the border pattern No. 7 When the demand for Traditional painting reduced she painted the Poppy range and then became Mary the chief checker of the finished pots coming from the kiln. Her sight was so good she could often find a blemish in a perfect piece! She was another very loyal character.

Pam Lane Pam could place a pot on a decorator's 'Banding Wheel', give it a tap and it was running perfectly true in the centre. I tried it many times and always failed. She painted bands around pots with effortless skill. It did not matter if the bands were wide or hairline thin they were always perfect. She could put the 'dots' on the top of Traditionally painted pots accurately and with the speed of a machine gun... As the need for hand painting declined she was involved in other decorating techniques. Ultimately she was our specialist with the offset pad printer. The Painters. Not already mentioned include Angela Hargreaves, Bridget Hillyard, Peggy Holman, Peggy Lay, and others noted in the Museum records.

Fettlers There were many over the years including May Crooke, Mary Denning, Jean Boyland (Ray's wife), Ivy Chivers, Debbie Howlett, Ruby Howard, Sheila Turner, Nora Cousins, Helen Larcombe, Carol Sexton and many others.

There was a team of up to six glaze sprayers working at any one time. They included, over the years, Arthur Long, Ray Boyland, Iris Meads, Julie Ward, Michaela Layzell, Dawn Manley, Lorainne Pye and Wendy Yeo, Joe Mc Cartney, and others. The glazes we mainly used were matt glazes, either the Traditional cream, Matt Brown or Devon Red. This was a skilled and very responsible job the importance of which could easily be overlooked. The quality of every product depended on them.

Lampshade making.   Jean Gigg as mentioned earlier became our expert and she was assisted by Val Boweren who also worked in the shop.

Bernard Hayman   I was told that he worked as a general Potter in the 1950s.   He returned in 1973 and took over as our packer.   He was very reliable, conscientious and efficient.   Not only did he take care of the pots but checked orders in detail and attended to the carriers.   He worked with Monica Wakeley our warehouse manager.

The shop and office in 1961 was initially up the driveway, well run by Grace Salter.   However when we purchased No. 30, High Street we moved the Offices and Shop into it.   The shop was a much enlarged area and more important operation so Grace took on the Shop full time.   Over the years the shop developed to include Nos. 32 and 34.   The staff included Frances Kreft, Gill Ellis, Val Bowern amongst others, and finally Marion Harris,   She managed the shop for many years. and somehow recognised and welcomed returning holiday makers even after a year or two.   The shop team were very important and were the people who made our many visitors very welcome. Marian Swan ran our office efficiently and well for many years.   She was a tower of strength and a lightning typist and tended many of our Trade show stands.   She looked after customers helpfully and with great tact..   Similarly the office had numerous people, Amanda Braddick, Dawn Carr, Ann Thomas, Valerie Cann, Diane Keightly, Shirley Wakeley and others.   They tolerated changes from simple double entry book keeping, to Kalamazoo, and eventually to computerisation run by Stella Webber.   We progressed from an Imperial typewriter to our first computer, an Olivetti with a 1K memory, and so to an Amstrad with 20K memory.   This at the time was state of the art technology and did everything we needed.   Accounts, letters, payroll, production control and company balance sheets were all run on it as well as our computer engraving machine.   What changes in computers since those days in the 1980s.

In 1973 there were more than sixty people on the payroll during the year including holiday and evening staff but the full timers were about forty.   In 1976 the total had dropped to about forty five on the payroll.   This reflected the change from hand decorated items to plain coloured glazes and pad printing.

It is difficult to imagine the wages when we first started in 1961. The pottery pay rates were quite good for the town.   The average paintresses earned 1/10d per hour and office staff 2/6p per hour in old money.   This is, in today's money, 9p or 12 .5p per hour.   How values have changed! Our grateful thanks to everyone who worked for us.

This

Appendix of
Honiton Pottery.

has a further selection of

colour sheets, silhouette sheets, pricelists
and other illustrations

that would have overpowered the text.

They are for information and reference purposes

to help identify other products made.

There are also copies of orders and other documents

which might be of interest to researchers.

PRICE LIST AND ORDER FORM

HONITON POTTERY LTD.

TEL. HONITON 106

DEVON   *BAND*

TRADITIONAL DECORATIONS   January 1, 1963

Article and Description	Decoration Number	Price each	Order	Remarks
4in. Jug Bicton	3 to 12	6/3		
6in. „ „	1 and 2	11/3		
6in. „ Lynton	„	12/6		
4in. „ Exton	3 to 12	4/9		
3in. „ Milton	3 to 12 & D/L	4/0		
4in. „ „	„	5/6		
5in. „ „	„	6/3		
3in. Vase Weston	Flower Spray	3/0		
3in. „ Manaton	3 to 12 & D/L	4/0		
3in. „ Rayton	„	4/0		
3in. „ Rinton	„	4/0		
4in. „ Denton	..	5/2		
5in. „ Cranton	2	5/0		
5in. „ Monkton	1 and 2	8/0		
6in. „ Ashton	„	10/9		
8in. „ Filton	„	14/6		
8in. „ Norton	„	15/0		
5in. „ Seaton	„	8/0		
6in. „ „	„	10/9		
10in. „ „	„	25/0		
9in. Carlton Bowl	„	28/6		
S/S Oval Dish	1 and 2	8/3		
L/S Oval Dish	„	14/6		
7in. Newton Dish	„	8/3		
9in. „ „	„	10/3		
6in. Posy Ring	3 to 12 & D/L	7/8		
4in. Posy Ring	„	5/3		
Posy Bowl	„	5/2		
S/S Posy Bowl	„	4/0		
Posy Boat	Flower Spray	3/3		
Cvd. Butter Dish, Eared	3 to 12 & D/L	8/3		
S/S Eared Butter Dish	„	4/4		
S/S Round Butter	8 to 12 & D/L	2/8		
L/S „ „	3 to 12 & D/L	3/2		
Cvd. Honey Jar	„	7/0		
Cvd. Preserve Jar	„	7/4		
3in. Two-handled Jar	„	8/3		
Condiment Set, Triple (no base)	..	12/6		
Condiment Set, Double (base)		8/3		

72

CRAFTSMAN

Oven to Tableware

PRICE LIST AND ORDER FORM
HONITON POTTERY LTD

HONITON-DEVON-ENGLAND EX14 8PU

TELEPHONE: HONITON   2106

Colours: Blue, Green, Amber, Matt-Brown, Devon-Red

Illust. No.	Article	Price	Order
1	5 pint Casserole	£1.60p	
2	3 pint Casserole	£1.38p	
2a	Cook 'n' Serve Casserole	£1.38p	
3	2 pint Casserole	£1.15p	
4	9in. Dish	64p	
4a	Divided Dish	90p	
5	Cov. Handled Soup	52p	
7	Casserole Warmer	86p	
8	4in. Butter Dish	13p	
8	6¼in. Plate	18p	
8	8½in Plate	30p	
8	9½in. Plate	36p	
8	10½in. Plate	40p	
8a	10½in x 8½in Oval Plate	36p	
8a	11½in x 9in Oval Plate	40p	
8b	12½in x 9½in Oval Platter	48p	
9	Cereal Bowl	26p	
10	Large Salt and Pepper	50p	
10a	Small Salt and Pepper	37p	
11	Sugar Shaker	35p	
12	Large Coffee Pot	90p	
13	Small Coffee Pot	75p	
14	Tea Pot	90p	
15	Cup and Saucer	40p	
16	Beaker and Saucer	41p	
16	Beaker	28p	
17	Sugar Bowl	25p	
18	Cream Jug	35p	
18a	Milk Jug	53p	
19	Egg Cup	17p	
20	Rectangular Butter Dish	50p	
21	Gravy Boat	36p	
22	Honey/Jam Pot	48p	

ALL PRICES QUOTED ARE SUBJECT TO PRICES RULING AT DATE OF DESPATCH AND ARE EXCLUSIVE OF PURCHASE OR OTHER TAX.

THE ABOVE PRICES INCLUDE THE COST OF THE CONTAINER AND CARRIAGE ON ALL ORDERS TO THE NET VALUE OF £30 AND OVER. ORDERS OF LESS THAN THIS VALUE WILL INCUR THE COST OF POSTAGE, CARRIAGE AND CONTAINER.

TRANSIT BREAKAGES MUST BE REPORTED TO THE CARRIER AND TO US WITHIN THREE DAYS, OTHERWISE NO RESPONSIBILITY CAN BE ACCEPTED FOR CLAIMS.

2½% SETTLEMENT DISCOUNT ALLOWED FOR PAYMENT WITHIN ONE MONTH FOLLOWING DATE OF INVOICE. 3¾% FOR CASH, SEVEN DAYS, OTHERWISE STRICTLY NET.

ORDER FROM...

....

....

DELIVERY...

DATE...

MAY 1st 1971

HONITON POTTERY LTD Honiton, Devon EX14 8PU Telephone: (0404) 2106

CRAFTSMAN
OVEN TO TABLEWARE

COLOURS: Banded Stoneware, Matt-Brown

C33	C34	C35	C40	C42
5 pt. Casserole	3 pt. Casserole	2 pt. Casserole	Rectangular Dish	Covered Dish
C01/02/03/04/27	C05/06	C07	C08	C09
Round Plates	Oval Plates	Oval Platter	Cereal Bowl	Large Cruet
C10	C14	C15	C16/17	C18/20
Honey Pot	Large Coffee Pot	Small Coffee Pot	Large or Small Teapot	Cup & Saucer
C19/20	C49	C21	C22	C23
Beaker & Saucer	Colony Coffee Mug	Haigh Beaker	Sugar Bowl	Cream Jug
C24	C25	C26	C28/29	C30
Milk Jug	Egg Cup	Butter Dish	Gravy Jug	Cheese Dish
C31	C74			
Oil & Vinegar	Sugar Shaker			

CONDITIONS OF SALE

All prices are subject to prices ruling at date of despatch and are exclusive of V.A.T. or other tax. The prices include the cost of the container and carriage on all orders to the net value of £100 and over. Orders of less than this value incur the cost of postage, carriage and container. Our minimum order charge is £20. Any order placed below this value will be charged as £20.

Transit breakages must be reported to the Carrier and to us within three days, otherwise no responsibility can be accepted for claims.

HONITON POTTERY LTD Honiton, Devon EX14 8PU Telephone:(0404) 2106

COOKWARE • OVEN-TO-TABLEWARE •
MICROWAVE OVENWARE • Part of our comprehensive range

C43 4" Flan Dish C44 8" Flan Dish   C45 9" Flan Dish   C46 10½" Flan Dish   C39 10" Hors D'oeuvre Dish

C47 Ramekin C50 6"x3" Soufflé C51 7"x4" Soufflé C52 8"x3" Soufflé   C53 Crescent   C48 Shell Dish

C49 Avocado Dish

C59 Baking Dish 9"x7"

C56 Baking Dish 10½"x8½"

C57 Baking Dish 11½"x9½"

C55 Small Oval Pie Dish

C58 Oval Baking Dish 10"x7¼"

C63 10" Storage Jar C64 7" Storage Jar C69 Salt Pig

C67 Large C65 Small C66 Medium
Stacking Jars

C70 Curved Store Jar

D59 Small Shire Trencher   D60 Large Shire Trencher

G85 18" Fish Platter

C32 Corn Cob Dish

G81 Lemon Squeezer

G82 1½ doz. Egg Hen   G83 1 doz. Egg Hen   G84 ½ doz. Egg Hen   G80 Egg Separator

TRADE PRICE LIST

JAN. 1977

VAT No. 140 7951 70.

HONITON POTTERY LIMITED

HIGH STREET, HONITON, DEVON. Tel: (0404) 2106

CONDITIONS OF SALE

All prices quoted are subject to prices ruling at date of despatch and are exclusive of V.A.T. or other tax.

The prices include the cost of the container and carriage on all orders to the net value of £75 and over. Orders of less than this value incur the cost of postage, carriage and container.

Our minimum order charge is £10. Any order placed below this value will be charged as £10.

Transit breakages must be reported to the Carrier and to us within three days, otherwise no responsibility can be accepted for claims. 2½% Settlement discount allowed for payment within 30 days following date of invoice.

CRAFTSMAN TABLEWARE RANGE

Matt Brown, Devon Red, Stoneware & Brushwork.

COLOURED			STONEWARE		BRUSHWORK	
Ref: No.	Price	Items	Ref: No.	Price	Ref: No.	Price
1001	£4.65	5 pt. Casserole	2001	£5.00	9001	£5.35
1002	3.33	3 pt. Casserole	2002	3.74	9002	3.82
1003	2.65	2 pt. Casserole	2003	2.91	9003	3.05
1004	1.49	1 Comp. Veg. Dish	2004	1.67	9004	1.71
1005	1.55	2 Comp. Veg. Dish	2005	1.70	9005	1.78
1007	1.35	Cov. Handled Soup	2007	1.50	9007	1.55
1008	.30	4″ Butter Dish	2008	.33	9008	.34
1009	.40	6¼″ Round Plate	2009	.44	9009	.46
1010	.66	8½″ Round Plate	2010	.74	9010	.75
1011	.87	9½″ Round Plate	2011	.97	9011	1.00
1012	.98	10½″ Round Plate	2012	1.09	9012	1.12
1013	.95	10½″ Oval Plate	2013	1.04	9013	1.09
1014	1.22	11½″ Oval Plate	2014	1.34	9014	1.40
1015	1.38	12½″ Oval Plate	2015	1.51	9015	1.58
1016	.52	Cereal/Soup Bowl	2016	.57	9016	.59
1017	.99	Large Salt/Pepper	2017	1.10	9017	1.14
1018	1.10	Large Mustard	2018	1.21	9018	1.26
1019	.74	Small Salt/Pepper	2019	.81	9019	.85
1020	.69	Small Mustard	2020	.76	9020	.79
1021	.80	Sugar Shaker	2021	.89	9021	.92
1022	9.00	Coffee Set — 15 Piece	2022	9.75	9022	10.40
1052	5.50	7 pc. Early Morning Set.	2052	6.00	9052	6.40
1023	2.47	Large Coffee Pot	2023	2.71	9023	3.12
1024	1.87	Small Coffee Pot	2024	2.06	9024	2.15
1025	2.99	Large Tea Pot	2025	3.25	9025	3.44
1026	2.47	Small Tea Pot	2026	2.71	9026	2.84
1027	.60	Cup	2027	.66	9027	.70
1028	.60	Beaker	2028	.66	9028	.70
1029	.29	Saucer	2029	.30	9029	.33
1030	.51	Sugar Bowl	2030	.56	9030	.58
1031	.83	Cream Jug	2031	.90	9031	.95
1032	1.35	1 pt. Milk Jug	2032	1.50	9032	1.55
1033	.40	Egg Cup	2033	.45	9033	.46
1034	1.38	Rect. Butter Dish	2034	1.50	9034	1.58
1035	.83	Gravy Boat	2035	.92	9035	.95
1036	1.10	Honey Pot	2036	1.21	9036	1.26
1037	2.19	Cheese Dish	2037	2.40	9037	2.52
1038	.94	Oil/Vinegar Bottle	2038	1.04	9038	1.08

COOKWARE RANGE

Available in White & Craftsman Range Colours

White			Coloured	
Ref: No.	Price	Item	Ref: No.	Price
6601	£1.15	8″ Flan Dish	6001	£1.25
6602	1.25	9″ Flan Dish	6002	1.50
6603	1.84	10½″ Flan Dish	6003	2.00
6610	.86	6″ x 3″ Souffle (1½ pt)	6010	.98
6611	1.15	7¼″ x 3½″ Souffle (2 pt)	6011	1.27
6612	1.27	8½″ x 3″ Souffle (2¼ pt)	6012	1.38
6621	.40	Small Oval Pie.	6021	.44
6622	1.40	Baking Dish 12″ x 6½″	6022	1.49
6623	1.45	Baking Dish 10½″ x 8½″	6023	1.60
6624	1.76	Baking Dish 11½″ x 9½″	6024	1.90
6634	2.50	Storage Jar	6034	2.65
6651	1.60	Rolling Pin	6051	1.80

Calman Cookery...
from Honiton Pottery.....

WHOLESALE TRADE PRICE LIST – JANUARY 1986

Made with LOVE, was it?

No- leftovers..

Ref No.	Article	PRICE PER ITEM One	Six
C44	*8" Flan Dish	£2.58	£2.48
C45	*9" Flan Dish	£3.29	£3.16
C51	7" x 3½" Souffle	£3.82	£3.65
C52	8" x 3" Souffle	£3.90	£3.70
C59	*9" x 7" Baking Dish	£3.38	£3.24
C56	*10" x 8" Baking Dish	£4.20	£4.02
C57	*11" x 9" Baking Dish	£4.98	£4.76
C58	10" x 7" Baking Dish Oval	£3.90	£3.70
G59	*Flora/Butter Holder	£3.06	£2.94

An assortment of designs will be supplied unless particular cartoons are requested.

The complete range is made to a high standard of Oven-to-Tableware and is suitable for general use in ovens including microwaves, and is dish-washer proof and made to B.S.4860

White glazed with red banded edge.   BOXED ITEMS *

Well?

If I say I liKED it - will you promise not to give it to me again?

CONDITIONS OF SALE

HONITON POTTERY LIMITED
30-34 High Street, Honiton, Devon
Telephone: Honiton (0404) 2106

Hand Painted
Honiton Pottery
GRAFFITI

P21	Norton Vase	£ 21.47	C16	Tea Pot	£ 21.33
P60	7" Plate	8.30	C18	Cup	6.08
G64	9" Plate	10.53	C20	Saucer	5.00
C84	Brunch Bowl	11.27	C23	Cream Jug	8.30
D32	B & L Soup Bowl	9.38	C22	Sugar Bowl	4.75
D30	B & L 8" Plate	7.70	G50	Devonmoor Mug	8.17
D31	B & L 10" Plate	10.13	G08	Small Mug	6.35
S09	Trinket Bowl	11.07	R68	Straight Mug	9.38

CONDITIONS OF SALE
All prices are subject to prices ruling at date of despatch and are exclusive of V.A.T or other tax. The prices include the cost of the container and carriage on all orders to the net value of £200 and over. Orders of less than this value incur a surcharge of £12 to cover the cost of postage, carriage and container. Orders of £20 net or less will be charged as £32 including carriage. These terms apply to U.K. mainland. Terms of payment 30 days net. Goods remain the property of the seller until fully paid for.

TRANSIT BREAKAGES must be reported to the Carriers and to us WITHIN 3 DAYS, otherwise no responsibility can be accepted for claims.

EXPORT TERMS: Orders over £600 F.O.B. British Port, otherwise ex-Works.

HONITON POTTERY LTD., 30-34, HIGH STREET, HONITON, DEVON EX14 8PU
HONITON (0404) 42106   TELEFAX (0404) 45119

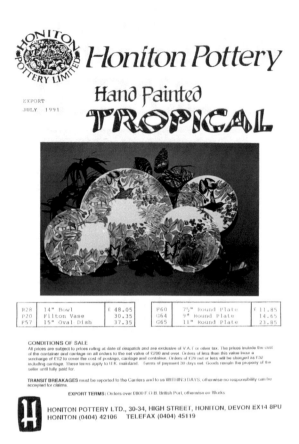

Honiton Pottery
Hand Painted
TROPICAL

P28	14" Bowl	£ 48.05	P60	7½" Round Plate	£ 11.85
P20	Filton Vase	30.35	G64	9" Round Plate	14.65
P57	15" Oval Dish	37.35	G65	11" Round Plate	23.85

CONDITIONS OF SALE
All prices are subject to prices ruling at date of despatch and are exclusive of V.A.T or other tax. The prices include the cost of the container and carriage on all orders to the net value of £200 and over. Orders of less than this value incur a surcharge of £12 to cover the cost of postage, carriage and container. Orders of £20 net or less will be charged as £32 including carriage. These terms apply to U.K. mainland. Terms of payment 30 days net. Goods remain the property of the seller until fully paid for.

TRANSIT BREAKAGES must be reported to the Carriers and to us WITHIN 3 DAYS, otherwise no responsibility can be accepted for claims.

EXPORT TERMS: Orders over £600 F.O.B. British Port, otherwise ex-Works.

HONITON POTTERY LTD., 30-34, HIGH STREET, HONITON, DEVON EX14 8PU
HONITON (0404) 42106   TELEFAX (0404) 45119

This is one of the more fun examples of a Collard plate, in the background, which we likes and used as a small range for the shop.

Chickens!

Tropical Range

Poppy Range

A selection of our Pottery Shop newspaper advertisements.

A selection of the artwork for our souvenir range.

Tower of London

The Strand, Calne.

Castle Combe, Wiltshire.

Gold Hill, Shaftesbury.

Stamford

Church Street, Calne, Wilts.

High Street, Honiton

TRESCO ABBEY GARDENS

Gold Hill, Shaftesbury.

Stamford

St.Mary Magdelene

Launceston.

City Hall, Belfast

Tower Bridge

BATH

Petts Wood

The Market Cross Malmesbury

St Paul's Cathedral

Salisbury Cathedral

81

Honiton Pottery
LETTER BOX
MONEY BOXES

		WHITE	RED	GREEN
R01	Penfold Victorian Letter Box	6.75	8.30	8.84
R02	Edwardian Pillar Box	5.80	7.29	--
R03	Georgian Post Box	3.92	5.20	--
R04	Redgrave Victorian Letter Box	6.75	8.30	8.84
R05	Crown & Cushion Letter Box	6.75	8.30	9.10
R06	S/S Edwardian Pillar Box	3.92	5.33	--
R07	S/S Penfold Letter Box	3.92	5.33	5.66

CONDITIONS OF SALE

All prices are subject to prices ruling at date of despatch and are exclusive of V.A.T or other tax. The prices include the cost of the container and carriage on all orders to the net value of £200 and over. Orders of less than this value incur a surcharge of £12 to cover the cost of postage, carriage and container. Orders of £20 net or less will be charged as £32 including carriage. These terms apply to U.K. mainland.   Terms of payment 30 days net. Goods remain the property of the seller until fully paid for.

TRANSIT BREAKAGES must be reported to the Carriers and to us WITHIN 3 DAYS, otherwise no responsibility can be accepted for claims.

EXPORT TERMS: Orders over £600 F.O.B. British Port, otherwise ex-Works.

HONITON POTTERY LTD., 30-34, HIGH STREET, HONITON, DEVON EX14 8PU
HONITON (0404) 42106   TELEFAX (0404) 45119

An example of some of the more interesting orders from special customers.

This order for tea mugs for Japan, the home of the Tea Ceremony, was a great delight and surprise.

SAZABY
LIVING
DIVISION

2-43, Higashi-Shinagawa
2-chome, Shinagawa-ku
TOKYO JAPAN 140
Telephone 03-474-5881/03-450-3993
Facsimile ████████/03-5479-4470
Telex J23627

TRANSMITTAL

DATE 30 January, 1992   TIME

TO   HONITON POTTERY   ATTENTION   Ms. Marian Swan

FROM Mika Ogita, Living Division

PROJECT   Our New Order   NUMBER OF PAGES   1 / 2

Dear Marian,

We would like to order you as the following items;

```
Devonmoor Mugs "Morning Cup"    Blue     2,770 pcs
     "          "Afternoon Tea"  Green    2,100  "
     "          "3 o'clock"      Brown    1,150  "
```

Delivery Time : at the middle of April, 1992
Shipping Agent: Escombe Lambert for Mitsui OSK Line as usual
Method of Payment: C.O.D. through our London Office

Please imput your producing schedule and advise us the new price.
And then, we will send you the correct our order sheet.

And also, we would like to know about the next page's our fax, if
you are available or not.

Looking forward to hearing from you soon.

Best regards,

Mika Ogita

If you are changed the Bank, please advise the new one.

Harrods.   All suppliers want to be represented here.

ORDER

See Conditions & Instructions Overleaf

Harrods
HARRODS LIMITED
KNIGHTSBRIDGE LONDON SWIX 7XL

974

TELEPHONE 01-730 1234 TELEX 24319 FAX 01 581 0470 REGISTERED OFFICE 87-135 BROMPTON ROAD, LONDON SW1X 7XL REGISTERED IN LONDON NO 30209

Fax 01-...

Telex 24319

VAT Registration No. 259 9768 79

Suppliers Code Number

Address for Delivery — Andree & Wilkerling

Mark X in appropriate box

		Half One	Half Two
Stock		101	102 α
Special		201	202
S.O.R.		301	302

Supplier's Name and Address:
Honiton Pottery
30-34 High Street
Honiton
Devon EX14 8PU

Settlement Terms
25% dis.

Quote this reference
→
on package and invoice

Order Number
B 21637 / 1400

Department No.

Buyer's Signature

Approximate Value C P T E   £874 —

Deliver first part	
Deliver second part	
Complete Delivery	asap 17 September 91

Date of Order

Day	Month	Year
2 1	0 8	9 1

Reference	Quantity				Unit Price	£	
	8	Penford Victorian – red	9"		8·30	66	40
	6	green	9"		8·84	53	04
	3	white	9"		6·75	20	25
	12	Edwardian Pillar – red	8½"		7·29	87	48
	3	white	8½"		5·80	17	40
	8	Redgrave Victorian – red	8½"		8·30	66	40
	8	green	8½"		8·84	70	72
	3	white	8½"		6·75	20	25
	8	Crown & Cushion – red	10½"		8·30	66	40
	8	green	10½"		9·10	72	80
	4	white	10½"		6·75	27	00
	4	Small – Georgian post 5" – white			3·92	15	68
	12	" red			5·20	62	40
	4	" – Edwardian Pillar 5" white			3·92	15	68
	12	" red			5·33	63	96
	4	" Penford Victorian 6" white			3·92	15	68
	12	" red			5·33	63	96
	12	" green			5·66	67	92

Form Number 0011

0085

Designed for use with a 'D.L.' window envelope. Fold at marker lines

873·42 REG

84

Cuthbertson.   The company was our largest customer for many years making their Christmas Tree range.

CUTHBERTSON LIMITED

P.O. BOX 3066 DARIEN, CONN. 0682_ _ A.
(203) 847-5752

Original Christmas Tree ®

	INVOICE NO. X X X
DATE	YOUR ORDER NO.
31 Jan. 1991	31/91

Alan G. Matthews
The Moorings
1 Elms Ave., Lilliput
POOLE, Dorset BH14 8EE

SOLD TO
Honiton Pottery Ltd.,
Honiton,
Devon,
EX14 8EX

SHIPPED TO
Prinknash Pottery,
Cranham,
Nr. Gloucester.

COUNTRY OF ORIGIN	PACKAGE NUMBERS	QUANTITY	DESCRIPTION		UNIT PRICE	NO. OF ITEMS PER INSIDE CARTONS	NO. OF ITEMS PER OUTSIDE CARTONS	TOTAL
			Original Christmas Tree - 1st Quality					
		480	C18 13" Oval Platter	4.14	4.05	½		1,944. 00
		1065	C19 11½" Oval Platter	3.02	2.97	1		3,163. 05
		150	C57 15" Oval Platter	5.90	5.83	1		874. 50
		185	C64 Cake Plate	3.30	3.24	1		599. 40
		430	C69 11½" Rect Platter	3.30	3.24	1		1,393. 20
		330	C70 13" Rect. Platter	4.34	4.27	1	2.43	1,409. 10
		150	C106 Devilled Egg Dish	2.47	2.31	1		346. 50
			Note:- All above to be packed individually for shipping direct to the USA.					
			For Sets					
		405	C19 - 11½" Oval Platters	3.02	2.97	Bulk		1,202. 85
			Note: Bulk pack and despatch to Prinknash Pottery for Sets (CPS6)					
								£10,932. 60

cc. Cuthbertson Imports
    Prinknash Pottery

| AMOUNT DUE | X X X |

PAYABLE IN
U.S. DOLLARS

85

Sundry additional pictures belatedly, randomly included.

"Uncle" Ron Finch preparing clay at our de-airing Pug Mill.

Edith Chapplow
Jennie Redvers
Nancy Hull

An example of the terracotta cookware.   It was a successful product but we discontinued the production after only a few weeks because the red clay could not be contained.   It contaminated the white clay.   Even a small amount in a machine, on a board or on a sponge left pinkish spots or streaks on the white pottery.   It was a shame to abandon an attractive product.

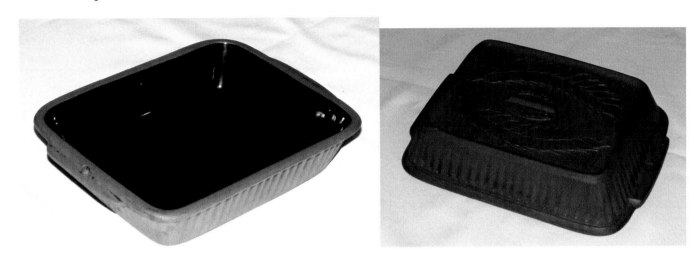

And finally memories of winter in the 1960s.

Glossary

of
Pottery terms

****

Also
Some details from Conveyances concerning the properties.

****

Which might be helpful.!
****

Glossary of some of the pottery terms used in the industry.

Biscuit   Pottery which has had one firing and is not glazed. It has the texture of dry biscuit.

Block moulds. The first mould made around the model of a pot being prepared for slip casting.

Blunger   A mixing tank for preparing clay as slip for casting.

Boards   Wooden planks, about 1 foot wide and usually 4 or 6 feet long, for carrying pottery on the shoulder around the works, traditionally used throughout the industry.

Bullers Rings Precision clay rings, like large washers, which are fired in the kiln to ensure the 'heat work' was correct during firing. They are measured on a special gauge. They are more accurate then Holdcrofts bars.

Case   The 'master' on which production slip casting moulds are made.

Clays   Clay has a flat, plate-like structure which allow it to slide and be 'plastic' when moistened with water. It contrasts with sand which has a crystal structure, like sugar grains, and does not become plastic.
China Clay is a primary clay, found where it is formed, geologically, in granite. It is less 'plastic' than secondary clays.
Red Clay, terracotta, is a secondary clay, formed by being washed down from the source into areas, such as river beds. Colour is due to iron oxide (rust) mixed in it.

China   A general term used for ceramic pieces. Bone China is a made of a ceramic clay mixed with calcined animal bone. The clay vitrifies in firing and becomes translucent.

Cones   Small cones of ceramic material designed to 'bend' at a particular temperature. Placed in a kiln to be observed through the 'Spy hole'. When they bend the kiln firing is complete.

Defloculation The breaking down of plastic clay into casting slip using Silicate of soda and soda ash.

Earthenware A standard term for pottery, when the clay has not been vitrified by the kiln firing. At Honiton both the red clay and the white clay were earthenware. This must have a glaze applied to make it non porous.

Fettling   Removing seams and blemishes from pottery with a knife or tool. (See pages 37 and 38).

Flannelling Wiping clean the 'foot' of pottery to remove raw glaze prior to placing in the kiln. This avoids the piece sticking to the kiln shelf.

Glaze   A form of glass with clay and a flux applied to pottery to seal the surface and for decorative reasons.
Lead Glaze contains lead used as a flux to adjust the glaze fusing temperature. Historically, Galena, a lead sulphide was used for glazing but can leach lead and be very poisonous. Now-a-days only low solubility lead compounds are used. Lead glazes have more sparkle than the alkaline mixtures.

Alkaline glaze. The main glaze flux system for all temperature glazes. Generally lacking high lustre which is why lead is used for low temperatures.

Matt glaze is a glaze which is modified so that it crystallises on cooling, changing the surface.

Tin glaze is an opaque milky white glaze with 10% tin oxide as used for Majolica and Delft ware.

Holdcroft bars Thermascope bars of an accurately mixed clay blend, designed to melt at a particular temperature. Usually three bars are placed as a set, two melting just below and one melting at the required temperature, are placed so that they can be seen through the kiln spy hole. Thus the Bottle kiln fireman knows when to stop the firing. Not needed with modern controls.

Jolly A type of automated pottery throwing wheel for round items, see page 34.

Kilns **Bottle kiln.** A coal fired kiln used at Honiton Pottery until 1953. see page 6
Electric Trolley hearth kilns, Loading and firing. See pages 18, 38and 39.

Kiln temperatures Observed through the 'Spy hole' or with a probe attached to an indicator dial, now-a-days a digital reader.
Colours seen through the spy hole. At about 600 degrees C. it glows a dull cherry red, at 1000 degrees C. it is orange (Earthenware), at 1200 degrees it is very bright orange (Stoneware), at 1500 degrees it is bluish white (Porcelain).

Moulds Working moulds for slip casting and for the Jolly are basically made of Plaster of Paris.

Master Block moulds are made of Plaster of Paris from the original model, tested, and then only used to make the "Case mould" and stored carefully.

Master Case moulds, from these the working moulds are made. They are made of a strong alpha plaster or sometimes now made in Resin or rubber.

Ram Press Moulds. Special moulds in steel frames for the press see page 35

Painting This is with metallic oxide mixtures such as cobalt for blue, iron and manganese for browns, copper and chrome for greens etc.
Under-glaze painting is applied on to the biscuit pots and then glazed.
On-glaze painting is applied on fired glaze.
In-glaze painting is applied on the raw glaze before firing.

Porcelain Very high fired vitrified ceramic, about 1500 degrees C. strong and often translucent.

Pug Mill A machine which cuts and blends plastic clay, usually with a vacuum system to ensure an air free mix, (De-airing Pug), extruding it ready for use. (Picture in the appendix)

Pyrometer A probe for kiln temperature measurement. (Usually platinum/rhodium)

Ram Press An hydraulic platen press with special features for pottery production. see pages 13 and 35.

Saggars   Large pottery containers, like large, old fashioned, hat boxes into which pottery was placed in 'Bottle' kilns.   This protected pots and was the method of stacking the kiln.

Silicate of Soda and Soda Ash.   The chemicals used to defloculate clay to create casting slip. They have to be used in combination to make an easily workable pot.   Alone Silicate of soda makes a 'flabby' pot and soda ash a dry and brittle pot.   Together success!

Slip   Clay in liquid form.   It may be simply clay mixed with water used to 'stick on' handles and knobs or specially prepared with soda ash and silicate of soda as required for 'slip casting'.

Sponging   Removing blemishes from pottery in combination with fettling. See pages 37 and 38. Sponging colour is sometimes used as a decoration technique.

Spy Hole   A small hole in the side of a kiln so that the inside of a firing kiln can be viewed. The Cones, Holdcroft Bars can be observed.

Stoneware A high fired ceramic about 1250 degrees C.   Vitrified pottery therefore does not need a glaze to seal the surface.   Usually earth colours typical of Bernard Leach's pottery.

Throwing (from the Anglo Saxon to spin or whirl) Making pottery on a potter's wheel.

Towing   Using a handful of 'tow', flax fibers, to remove blemishes and round the edges of dry, unfired clayware plates set on a motorized wheel. A dusty process now replaced by wet sponging.

Transfers Ceramic transfers, widely used in the industry for decorating ceramics. Water slide from gummed paper using special ceramic colours. Usually fired at 750 degrees C.

Turning   Trimming the base of a thrown pot, on a potter's wheel or lathe, to create a 'foot' and/ or to decorate a pot.

Pottery Records from Deeds and Documents
held at Everys, Solicitors, Honiton.

Purchase of " The Old Pottery site" . Document relates to Nos. 16,18 and 20 High Street and the land behind Nos. 20 to 28 High Street.
27 May 1950 Mr. Slade deceased to Mrs. Slade. "The Old Pottery ,former Kiln buildings ... comprising Tithe numbers 719, 720, 722, 723 and 724.

Conveyance 14th June 1976 to Honiton Pottery Ltd. of part of Number 3665 on the O.S. Map.

Conveyance Dated 22nd March 1922
Indenture Mrs. Sophia Ann Ackling to Charles Collard.
The Pottery site behind No. 32 (Henrietta Cottage later known as Montpellier) and 34 High Street and the entranceway between No. 30 and No. 32.

This was left by Richard Sprague, father of Ellen Webber in a Will of 7th. June 1883 gave Henrietta Cottage to Ellen Webber and the walled garden at the back of the house and the large linney at the back of Mr. Oake's garden.   James Webber, husband of Ellen, is given certain rights in the Will.
Ellen died on the 28th July 1897   Her Will was never proved.
Joseph Walter made his Will on the 28th Nov. 1904
James Webber died on 13 April 1920.
No date when Collard started here but it says "the site now used as a pottery and in the occupation of the purchaser."

Conveyance dated 11th August 1928
Dwelling house Kingswood 30 High Street
From Walter Howard to Charles Collard

 It noted that:-
Conveyed to Honiton Art Potteries Ltd.   12th June 1947

Deed of Assignment 12 June 1947
Dwelling house Kingswood 30 High Street
From Charles Collard to The Honiton Art Potteries Ltd.
The Directors Edyth Chapplow, and Mr. & Mrs. Hull

Sale of the Goodwill of the business for £5,100 , being £3,100 for the plant stock etc.

Indenture 21 July 1924
Dwelling house Kingswood 30 High Street
From Ethel Maud Parrett to Walter Howard for £600
